KENT SEAWAYS

Hoys to Hovercraft

Michael Langley

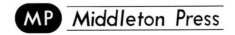
MP Middleton Press

Front cover pictures: Top left -   The "Hoy" **GOOD INTENT** see caption 77
                         Top right -   **PS MEDWAY QUEEN** see caption 91
                         Lower left -   **SS FORDE** see caption 165
                         Lower -   **SIR CHRISTOPHER** see caption 127

Back cover pictures: Top -   **SIRDAR** see caption 35
                         Lower -   **STENA INVICTA** see caption 178

Notes about the Author-

Childhood visits to the Sussex ports from his Horsham birthplace, and family gatherings cross-Solent on the Isle of Wight, kindled an early interest in shipping. Holidays in the Romney Bay area of South Kent were similarly influential. After Navigation School a career in deep sea shipping ensued with the P & O Group. Visits to the Medway, whilst serving with Trident Tankers Ltd; were not uncommon and a camera was often to hand. The shipping career finally ended after a number of years, 'navigating a desk' at Head Office, as a Marine Superintendent in Ship Management. Redundancy, in the early 1990s led to a move to the Isle of Wight, renewed interest in coastal shipping history, research, and a turn to writing. 'Kent Seaways' follows **'Sussex Shipping- Sail, Steam & Motor'** and **'Solent- Creeks, Craft & Cargoes'**.

Published June 2006

ISBN 1 904474 79 9

© Middleton Press, 2006

Design Deborah Esher

Published by
          Middleton Press
          Easebourne Lane
          Midhurst, West Sussex
          GU29 9AZ
Tel: 01730 813169
Fax: 01730 812601
Email: info@middletonpress.co.uk
www.middletonpress.co.uk

Printed & bound by Biddles Ltd, Kings Lynn

CONTENTS

PREFACE

There were few options for the movement of goods in the pre-railway era. Volumes of course were low, but roads dangerous and often impassable. Plentiful supplies of timber would ensure that local shipbuilding and waterborne transportation flourished in the tidal creeks, rivers and harbours of North Kent. East Kent's proximity to Continental Europe has encouraged continual port development to serve ever expanding trade and traveller numbers. After all, the Romans and others have chosen the narrow part of the English Channel for their landing, in preference to a longer more exposed and riskier sea crossing, in uncharted waters. Today, the majority of the smaller commercial craft described herein are but a memory. Most modern freight travels 'door to door' courtesy of the giant roll-on, roll-off ferries, or deep sea by large containership. Few minor ports now witness commercial shipping activity, the vacancies resulting being partly offset by yachts, their marinas and the leisure industry.

GLOSSARY & ABBREVIATIONS

------	Sailing Ships / un-powered craft		PT	Paddle Tug
MB	Motor Barge		SS	Steam Ship
MFV	Motor Fishing Vessel		ST	Steam Tug / Steam Trawler
MT	Motor Tanker / Motor Tug		THV	Trinity House Vessel
MV	Motor Vessel		TSS	Twin Screw Steam Ship
PS	Paddle Steamer		TSMV	Twin Screw Motor Vessel

Tonnages:

Gross Registered Tonnage, abbr. **grt**:-g- volumetric measure of all enclosed space applied to all ships. 100 cu.ft. = 1 gross ton. This is the true indicator of the ship's overall size.

Net Registered Tonnage, abbr. **nrt**:-n- sometimes shown as reg. tons, - r- probable original derivation from sailing ship days in the wine trade when 'tuns' implied barrel capacity of 252 gallons, per barrel. ie. the earning capacity volume.

Deadweight Tonnage, abbr. **dwt**:- the actual weight carrying capacity of the ship in tons, includes fuel, water, stores etc; plus cargo.

Form used in captions – eg;   199g/1960 ------a ship of 199 gross tons, built in 1960

Length overall:	loa	Measurement to the fore and aft extremities
Beam or breadth:	br	Measurement to the maximum width
Draught:	dr	Depth of water required for flotation

Horse Power, engines:-

NP	Nominal Horse Power
IP	Indicated Horse Power
SHP	Shaft Horse Power - usually given for steamships.
BHP	Brake Horse Power - usually given for motor vessels.

Knots/kt:	Speed in nautical miles (6080 ft.) per hour.
Spring Tides:	fortnightly periods of greater tidal range - 'higher' high water and 'lower' low water.
Neap Tides:	intervening periods of lesser tidal range - 'lower' high water and 'higher' low water.

INTRODUCTION

The commercial shipping activity examined may be considered to fall into two distinct geographic areas. The first consists of the traffic of the North Kent Coast with its charming historic ports and navigable creeks. To this may also be added the forty odd mile navigation of the River Medway inland to Tonbridge, plus the Medway Estuary, with its modern deepwater facilities for ocean going trade, still very economically important, today.

Secondly, the East Kent Channel ports between North Foreland and Dungeness Point, by virtue of their location have seen vast changes in utilisation. This section of the book highlights in particular the evolution of the ships, their trade and harbour developments with regard to cross-Channel traffic. The mere twenty or so miles of water across the Dover Strait has witnessed failed, and one or two successful invasions, and a continuous expansion of goods transported, and traveller numbers, over two thousand years.

In a less technological age, all ships were totally subject to the vagaries of wind, tide and currents. Losses in the days of sail were commonplace. The proximity of that well known ship-trap, the Goodwin Sands to this arterial seaway, where all shipping bound up or down Channel must pass, led to countless mishaps and disasters. The seamen of Deal, Ramsgate and Dover were called out to innumerable rescues and salvage operations, often in atrocious conditions. Their bravery and fine seamanship knew no bounds.

Today the large roll-on, roll-off ferries are merely sea-going extensions to Europe's motorway network, a function they uphold together with the Channel Tunnel. Freight now travels thousands of miles without intermediate handling at the ports. Excepting dry and liquid bulk commodities, and items unsuited to the 'boxes', most ocean trade is similarly containerised.

The book is interspersed with various local maps to aid the reader's navigation, and some longer descriptive sections highlight particular historic and local subjects. Our voyage begins inland at Tonbridge on the fresh water River Medway, and terminates in the salty environs of Dungeness, where we will 'drop the Pilot'.

Despite the success of the Channel Tunnel and its undoubted effect on traffic patterns, the United Kingdom will always be a collection of offshore islands. Ninety four percent of freight still continues to move by sea.

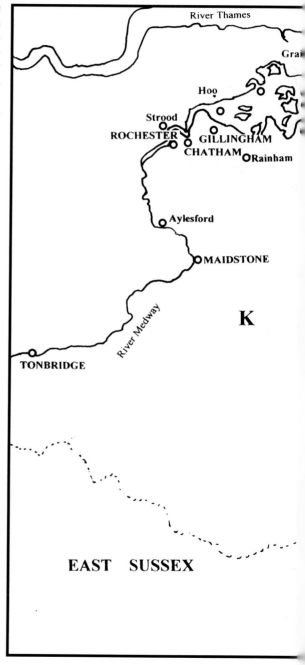

River Thames

Gra

Hoo

Strood

ROCHESTER   GILLINGHAM

CHATHAM ORainham

Aylesford

MAIDSTONE

K

River Medway

TONBRIDGE

EAST   SUSSEX

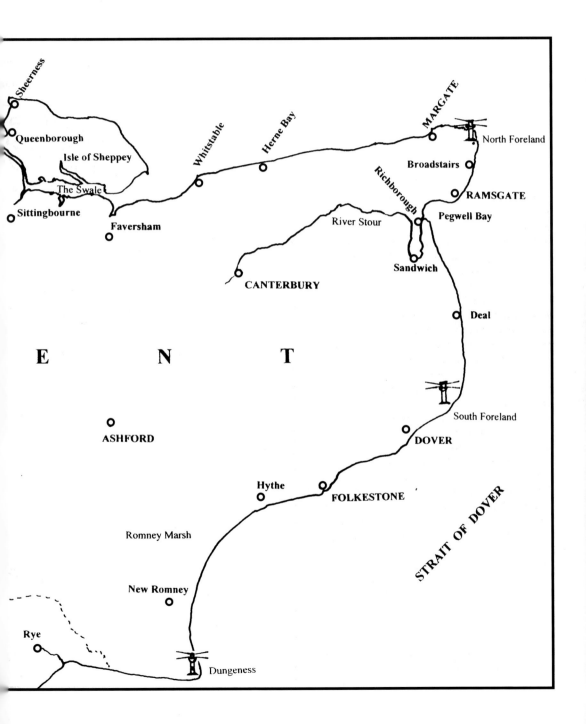

Map No.1   River Medway, Tonbridge to Maidstone

(1)   Tonbridge, Great Bridge, seagoing barge navigation limit.

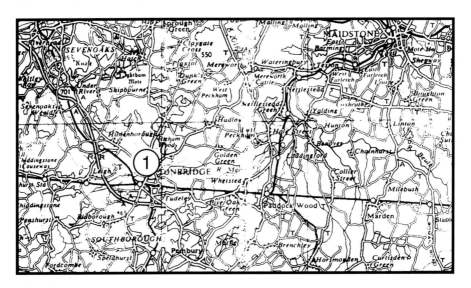

1.   SAMUEL, at Tonbridge →

Three sailing barges and a lighter are seen here working cargo at Medway Wharf, Tonbridge in the early 1900s. Gang planks, wheel barrows and man power predominate in the traditional manner. Sawn timber would often be dropped overboard deliberately and many ports around the Country had timber 'storage' ponds - some even in salt water. The 1892 45reg. ton *Samuel* was built at Sittingbourne and owned there by Wills & Packham Ltd. Barely a ripple disturbs this industrial scene, some forty three miles from the open sea. Barges of 100 to 120 tons capacity could reach Tonbridge from the 1740s, after various downstream river improvement works. Smaller local river barges could operate several miles further upstream in the 1800s, to serve such places as Leigh Gunpowder Mills. Commercial traffic dwindled until cessation at Tonbridge in the 1920s.

2.   Medway Wharf, Tonbridge →

The Medway still placidly flows past the earlier scene of such activity. Today in 2005 converted warehouses and purpose built smart homes line the bank. Trees appear to have long since re-asserted their long lost authority in this view downstream from the Great Bridge.

3. Tonbridge, Town Lock

Two typical 'Medway' open lighters lie below the lower lock gates. Both would appear to be ex seagoing barges cut down for the lighterage work, as each has two hatchways. They both exhibit the extraordinarily long rudders and tillers of their day. The inboard craft is *Sarah* of Rochester. The outer barge has the type of narrow stern typical of the 1860s. The photograph dates from the early 1900s and both craft have their registration numbers carved on their transoms.

4. The Lock in 2005 →

Grass thrives where the feet of many bargemen trod to prevent its establishment. The lock has been totally rebuilt and re-piled, with a landing stage for pleasure boat users that would have astonished the bargees, unaccustomed to such facilities.

5. BRITANNIA at Maidstone →

A lighter lies empty alongside a small group of sailing barges just above Maidstone Bridge in the 1920s. The timber laden barge is *Britannia* 45r/1883 and built by R.M.Shrubshall. The inner barge is the *Cryalls* 38r/1870 and also built at Milton. From ocean going vessels to humble barges popular names have been repeated many times over the years. Traffic at Maidstone consisted of coal, hops, stone, timber, beer and agricultural produce. General goods arrived by a number of regular barge services from London. Gasworks coal continued to be barged in until works closure in 1967. As we have seen, the sixteen miles above this point to Tonbridge became accessible after lock building works, just below Maidstone and at points above the town in the 1700s. A major traffic was the servicing of Brantbridges Mill at East Peckham. The paper mills at Tovil were barge supplied until 1977.

6. CARLOTTA at Maidstone

Bridge Wharf, Maidstone in the 1920s and the nearest vessel is *Carlotta* 44r/1892. She has evidently just arrived with a good deck load of sawn timber, probably from the Baltic and trans-shipped from a steamer in the Surrey Commercial Docks, London. This barge ended her trading days for the London & Rochester Company, whose name, and importance to the area, will be much touched upon in the pages to follow.

7. Maidstone in 2005 ↗

An enclosed 'tripper' boat is moored and awaits patrons, for a pleasant river cruise. Apart from the lack of working barges, the scene remains little altered over the century. Maidstone saw sailing barge construction in some numbers, eg; *Albert* 50r/1906, *Alice* 50r/1895, *Delta* 41r/1898, *Enchantress* 65r/1908, and *Gonda* 40r/1912. Later, A. Hutson built *Marie May*, *Mousme* and *Thyra* towards the end of barge building around the 1920s. Stone quarries just downstream of Maidstone generated much waterborne traffic - Bensteads sent away barge loads of 'ragstone' used in road building and tarmacadam - a cargo much loathed by barge crews, was a regular London bound freight, loaded nearby.

8. ST MEDWAY

A 'sylvan' setting near Maidstone in the 1920s, and a Walter Dowsett photograph has the little steam tug *Medway* 30g/1895 towing a barge with gear lowered. This tug was built at Canning Town, and, in 1904, came under Rochester registration and J.P. Knight ownership. Iron and steel hulled, 20HP could be mustered, and stately progress would be required to avoid damaging wash to the Medway's banks. The skipper's cap is shielding his eyes from the sun. The mast and funnel hinges would see more action before clearing Rochester's bridges.

← 9.   ALICE at Allington Lock

Seen here awaiting entry to the lock in the 1930s is the London & Rochester Company's *Alice* 50r/1895 and not far from her birthplace. Her sailing gear is part raised and there would be periodic cranking of the hand windlass either side of bridges, if wind was there to be caught, in between.

← 10. 1935 Floods at Allington

Three laden barges' progress has been seriously interrupted and they await the retreat of the floods before resuming their journey. It was as a result of such serious flooding that major improvement works were undertaken at Allington, to help alleviate any future problems. In 1937, new vertical, counterweight electrically controlled gates replaced the old sluices. Two barges are identifiable here - nearest is *Five Sisters* 41r/1891. The next one is *Redshank* 35r/1903.

11.   Allington Lock in 2005

Although navigable to some degree for centuries to Maidstone, the construction of the first lock here just after 1800, rendered the waters above non-tidal. This enabled craft working on up to Maidstone and Tonbridge, to remain afloat at all times with unrestricted movement possible. The lock was enlarged in 1880. A number of authorities have variously been responsible for the river over the years, including The Medway Conservancy, River Medway Catchment Board, Southern Water Authority and The Environment Agency. The tideway downstream came under the Medway Ports Authority jurisdiction. In this photograph the seaward lock gates are open, whilst to the right beyond the neatly clipped hedge, the main volume of Medway water flows by, having just been through the floodgates. The barges are long gone- their ultimate replacement in the form of 'juggernaut' trucks may be seen off to the right, thundering along the motorway.

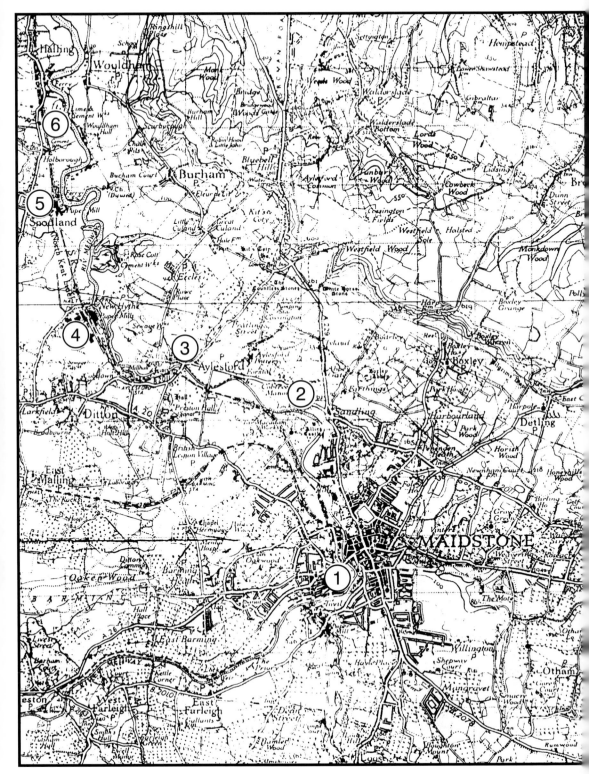

← Map No.2   Maidstone to Halling

(1)   Timber Wharf
(2)   Allington Lock
(3)   Aylesford Bridge
(4)   New Hythe Paper Mills
(5)   Snodland Paper Mill
(6)   Holborough Cement Works

Tidal Medway

The river from Allington Lock down to Rochester Bridge has seen a high degree of industrialisation with the associated rise and fall of many local enterprises. Benefitting from an abundance of chalk and other quarried commodities, industry soon exploited such riches to the full, all making good use of waterborne transport.

One major player was Reed's, New Hythe Paper Mills, some seven miles upstream from Rochester. In the peak years of newsprint production some 350,000 tons a year was rolled out, by some 3,500 employees. China clay, essential in the process was barged up-river after transhipment from larger steamers downstream, or by small motor coaster direct from the Cornish clay ports.

Pulpwood, similarly arrived from Canada, The United States of America and Scandinavia. Thousands of tons of coal per week were required to power the whole process. Finished newsprint would then be barged back downstream for export, etc. Numerous cement works opened between Snodland, Halling and Cuxton, and as individual quarry pits expired, others soon opened nearby. Some works produced lime. All were dependent on the waterway for their livelihoods, although this would wane as more works became siding connected to the railway system. Apart from the Capital's great appetite for cement, a large quantity found its way to many destinations around the Country.

12.   Aylesford Bridge and barges 1900s

A 14th century bridge was replaced around 1800 with this larger arched stone version, to aid navigation. The wharf here saw much local traffic and in this scene a group of three barges are being attended to by the customary horses and carts. The George Hotel overlooks bustling activity. Aylesford saw the construction of some sailing barges up until the 1880s, eg; *Arthur Margetts* 43r/1885, *October* 40r/1876, and *Tuesday* 42r/1883. Local sandpits and mills together with agricultural cargoes, provided the waterborne trade.

13. Aylesford Bridge in 2005 →

One hundred years later and a kind of 'genteel elegance' has displaced commercial life. An attractive shrub garden lies between the old Hotel and an overgrown wharf. Apart from the comings and goings of individual tree specimens, the scene remains largely unaltered. Any mariner wishing to moor here nowadays, would be well advised to check for boulders or 'dead' bicycles, before so doing.

Map No.3   Halling to Gillingham

(1) Strood Dock
(2) Frindsbury Peninsula
(3) Chatham Historic Dockyard
(4) Area of old Naval Basins
(5) Upnor
(6) Hoo Marina

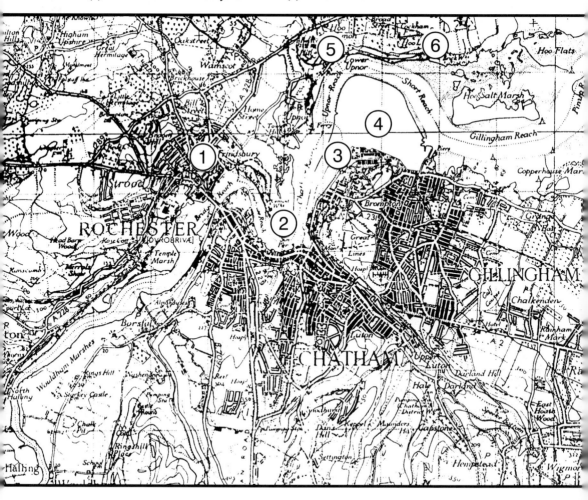

14. Rochester Bridges around 1910

Careful observation here shows much detail. A laden sailing barge has just 'shot' the bridge, and her crew will be frantically cranking that hand windlass to raise the sailing gear, en route up-river. A couple of grey hulled steamers are just visible working cargo on Strood Buoys. Innumerable barges are scattered about evidenced by their distinctive sprit rig. A distant smoke haze hangs over the industrial area of Strood Dock and Frindsbury, whose Church presides on the hill top. Incidentally, spritsail rigged barges somehow manage to confirm their presence in no less than forty of this book's illustrations - such was their importance to the region!

15. 'Raising the gear'

This is the reverse view to No.14. A deeply laden barge bound upriver has just 'shot' -passed under - the bridge, from which, no doubt the scene was photographed. The crew normally would have an additional helper onboard for this moment, as speed was of the essence in restoring the craft's sailing ability. This barge appears to have more than one helper, as no less than three boats trail astern - the gear should be swiftly back into sailing mode. Once the breeze is back in the sails the two man crew will be on their own again. 'Shooting' the Thames and Medway bridges on the tide required supreme judgement and skill in un-powered craft, long lost in our motorised times.

Sailing Barges

Thames and Medway barge evolution has surely been one of the more thoroughly researched and recorded forms of water transportation. The hull type encompassed the shallow, flat bottomed, box-like form of earlier small river and canal traders. This was gradually blended with that of stouter, more heavily constructed, sea-going 'hoys'. These deeper draughted vessels had carried cargo and passengers, and were single masted having seen little alteration since the early 1500s. Dutch influence in sailing barge design cannot be ruled out, as their early rig, leeboards and shallow draught had evolved to cope with similar waterways.

Incremental design changes in the 1700s saw the general introduction of that spritsail rig and leeboards to our barge fleet. Still steered by tiller, it would not be until the 1880s that wheel steering grew in popularity. Additionally rigs increased sail carrying ability and the characteristic long bowsprit became commonplace.

By around 1900, barge numbers had peaked at just over two thousand. Cargo capacity ranged from less than 100 tons up to about 150, yet the ultimate sailing barge design for the longer distance coastal traders would, in the 1920s, enable a lift well in excess of 250 tons. Their area of operation extended well beyond the Thames, Kent and Essex, to the North Sea Coasts, near Continental ports and the English Channel. Steel hulls became popular from the 1890s with some barge owners.

The railway era seemingly enhanced barge activity, as many local wharves became rail connected, they provided barge employment for their servicing. By the middle of the 20th century, auxiliary motor power reliability improved, and slowly at first, barge owners began to fit such engines to their craft. That age old reliance on the fickle wind was passing into history. Many barges thus converted traded on as 'auxiliaries' for a decade or two after WWII, by which time, alas, road transport had largely purloined their traditional freights.

In the 1950s and 1960s, a number of purpose built replacement motor barges came into service. Their size still permitted access to many of the old barge haunts, but in reality this new breed of efficient tiny motor coasters could still not reverse the trend to road haulage. Most ceased trading by the year 2000, save for a few in the age old sand and ballast trade.

Some examples of cargoes carried by the sailing barges:

Beer, bricks, cattle cake, cement, chalk, chemicals, china clay, coal, coke, cotton, explosives, flints, flour, general goods, grain, gravel, ground nuts, hay, lime, linseed, manure, mud, monkey nuts, paper, pitch, rootcrops, sand, stone, straw, tarmacadam, timber and woodpulp.

16. BEMBRIDGE at Rochester

In this Springtime 2005 view a couple of interesting craft lie at a Strood pontoon mooring. The ex Trinity House pilot tender *Bembridge* 413g/1938 has just ended her second career as a 'club-house' at Leigh-on-Sea, Essex and awaits her fate. The tiny upper Thames tug *Sheen* 48g/1925 and once a steamer, started life with Tough & Henderson. Both have done well to survive beyond the year 2000. *Bembridge* has long been devoid of her funnel. This scene is reverse to No.14 of ninety years earlier.

← 17. SS WHEELSMAN

Dutch built in 1920, this 1,394 grt steamer was the last dry cargo ship in owner C. Rowbotham's fleet. Throughout the twenties and up to 1935, she carried Blue Circle cement from the Medway to the Mersey. Subsequently Rowbothams went entirely over to the operation of coastal tankers, continuing to trade under various 'parent' groups until recently. In this unknown location photograph, (possibly Merseyside), the ship is locking-out with a couple of steam coasters. Note the ship's name carved on the wooden emergency steering wheel box, on the poop; also just visible, the 'Blue Circle' logo on the funnel.

← 18. Strood Dock and SS CONDOR

The Higham Canal and Tunnel opened in 1824 thus permitting barge sized craft to travel from Thames to Medway without putting to sea around the Isle of Grain. Railway records state the tunnel to be of 3,900 yards in length. As barge traffic soon increased, queues began to form at either end, so the Canal Company duly dug a deep rock cutting 200ft. down from the hill top to the canal at approximately mid length. A 50 yard passing place for barges was constructed. Craft up to 100ft loa and 18ft br by 5ft draught could navigate through. In 1844 the Gravesend & Rochester Railway Company pushed a single track line through the canal tunnel, partly on the tow-path and partly on piles driven into the waterway. Such drastic modifications were of course the death knell for the canal - cohabitation was just not on the agenda. In 1847 the Railway Company duly filled in the canal, and doubled the track. To this day the tunnel serves in its railway capacity almost 200 years after construction. Strood Dock handled coal, stone, clay and fertiliser cargoes before finally closing in 1962. After in-filling it now supports a housing estate. In the 1920s photograph, the identifiable steam coaster on the right is the Belgian SS *Condor* 410g/1918 and built at Vlaardingen. She displays the old name for Antwerp as her registration port 'Anvers', on the stern.

19. Strood Dock entrance in 2005

In the immediate foreground stands a line of corrugated steel piling, and behind the camera lies the old dock site, described in No.18. The outer lock gate and railway tunnel are the only survivors of this once important industrial site. To the right beyond the shrubbery along Canal Road, such premises as British Oil & Cake Mills, Barnetts Wharf, Cranfields Flour Depot, Horsnails & Reynolds (seed merchants) and Drakes Timber Yard once traded - all duly attended by waterborne transport. BOCM imported linseed in bags from steamers in the London Docks— sending out manufactured cattle cake coastwise to such locations as Hull.

← 20. SS FINNMAID

Strood buoys, just below Rochester Bridge have long been the up-river limit for fixed masted seagoing vessels on the River Medway. It therefore has featured as a trans-shipment point for goods to and from the upper reaches via lighters and barges. In this interesting photograph from the 1950s, one of the last steam powered cargo ships of its size to be built, SS *Finnmaid* 2,286g/1956, has her hatch tarpaulins raised to ward off a shower. Owned in Finland by Finnlines, this ship was powered by a four cylinder steam engine. A near sister ship had motor propulsion. Finnlines ordered no more of the steam powered variety. The lighters' cargo alongside seems unprotected as they await completion, whilst a group of 'ever hopeful' fishing lads are slightly hampered by the presence of the London & Rochester Company's tug *Enticette* 108g/1953, moored alongside Strood Pier.

← 21. MVs LODELLA and BRENDA PRIOR

Two little coastal motor vessel types seen here in 2005 are the ex. L&RTCo's *Lodella* 200g/1971, and *Brenda Prior* 198g/1968, ex L&RTCo. *Kiption*. Both are still trading locally in the sand and ballast business, in effect, modern descendants of the sailing barges. Today, just a handful of similar sized craft remain in service. *Brenda Prior* is receiving attention at the old Acorn Shipyard site on the Rochester side of the river.

22. PS KINGSWEAR CASTLE

Astern from Strood Pier in 2005 goes the delightful ex River Dart paddle steamer *Kingswear Castle* 94g/1924 now operating a series of summer cruises on the Medway, her home for some decades. The little coal burning steamer has just acquired a new forward covered companionway to the lower saloon, slightly altering her profile. Beyond lies what once would have been the menacing sight of a Russian Foxtrot class submarine-U475 of 1972. Previously she had been open to the public at Folkestone and now awaits her fate on Strood buoys. In the middle distance another ex L&RTCo. motor barge is drawn up on the Quarry Yard slipway. To the right and fronting Limehouse Reach, the wharves on the Frindsbury Peninsula side now form Rochester's commercial port.

23. PS MEDWAY QUEEN

Here the well known paddle steamer 316g/1924 has just left Strood Pier around 1960, with a good number of excursion passengers for the day's outing. Beyond lies the Company's Acorn Shipyard. This two cylinder steamer came from the Ailsa Shipbuilding Company at Troon, in Scotland. Taken out of service in the early 1960s, the ship spent some years on the River Medina in the Isle of Wight, before transportation on a barge back to the Medway. Today, restoration work progesses at a berth a few miles downstream at Damhead Creek, courtesy of the Medway Queen Preservation Society. Her original owners, The New Medway Steam Packet Company operated a number of paddlers and became part of the General Steam Navigation Company in 1936. That firm itself had been under the P & O banner since 1920. Later the Acorn Shipyard would be run by Lapthorns and Union Transport, and as we have seen in No.21, it survives as a repair facility, today. Other well known names hereabouts include J.P. Knight - tugs and towage, Thomas Watson - sailing barges through to modern motor coasters, Short Brothers (Aircraft), of Rochester - turned their attention to some barge building eg., *Lady Daphne*, *Lady Jean* and MB *Rochester Castle*.

24. PS CITY OF ROCHESTER →

Another popular unit of the NMSPCo. fleet was this paddler built in 1904 and of 235 grt. Standing alone at the wheel of his unprotected bridge, the smartly uniformed master really does look the part. Indeed, officer and crew appearance on some excursion paddlers would outdo many of their deep sea liner counterparts, in smartness terms. The photograph dates from around 1930.

25. MV BRAGA →

This bright green hulled ultra modern cargo ship is of a type evolved in recent decades known as LAD's. This stands for low air draught, enabling relatively large vessels to carry cargoes way inland on Europe's waterway systems, yet still able to trade deep sea. *Braga* 1,921g/2003 is Portuguese owned and Madeira registered. The simple masts can fold flat, and the wheelhouse perched on its rectangular section base, can be lowered for the ship to be 'conned' from deck level. Hatches are of the slab type, lifted on and off by a rail mounted gantry crane, which can be seen poised to lift and close the last two slabs in this 2005 photograph.

26. MV SCOT VENTURE

A recent and rare success story in British shipping has been that of Scotline of Inverness, who are much involved in the timber products trade. Seen here in 2005 at the Company's Rochester terminal, in Limehouse Reach is *Scot Venture* 3,300 dwt/2002. She relies on shore cranes for cargo work and has the same hatch system as No.25. The ship's overall layout is conventional and she is registered at Inverness.

27. 'Lash' rice barges

The local tug *Argonaut* waits patiently alongside pairs of yellow painted 'Lash' rice barges. These are part of a lighter aboard ship, ocean going transport system, and will duly be towed down river to a deep water mooring where they will be placed aboard the 'mother'ship, for the ocean voyage. Bulk rice for the processing plant beyond comes from places such as New Orleans, USA. The rice discharging equipment can be seen on the quayside above the tug. This 2005 scene is on the Frindsbury side of Chatham Reach.

28. 'Over the Dockyard wall' →

When taken, there was no intention to make this a puzzle image. Here we can see two of the three square rigged masts and slender funnel of HMS *Gannet*, a sail and steam Naval sloop dating from 1878. She is now open to the public and resides in an old drydock at Chatham. Closer to the camera stand a brand new pair of paddle boxes, and a new funnel for the previously mentioned PS *Medway Queen*. The items are perched on the dock wall - the ship herself lies a few miles downstream awaiting unification with her new components, during restoration work.

29. PT JOHN H. AMOS

A rather sadder image is that of the River Tees Conservancy's 1931, 202 grt paddle tug. Built very late for such a type, she has a 126HP, 4 cylinder steam engine and measured 110ft loa by 22ft br. Subject to various calls for restoration over the years, evidently to date funding has eluded her. Another candidate for a new funnel, at least! She lies just outside the old Naval Base, on the Medway's banks. Although this book makes no attempt to describe naval vessels, a brief local history note here, may not be amiss. Chatham Royal Naval Dockyards were established around 1547 and finally closed in 1983. Basin No.3 was put into commercial cargo use by 1985.

← 30. ARETHUSA and CAMBRIA

Upnor once held the Naval Ordnance Depot, a public pier and the APCM barge moorings and yard. Patman's Wharf once exported foundry sand. The two subjects of this fine 1972 study, courtesy of the Kent Messenger, come from the days when sailing ships could still earn money in both coastal and ocean trades. At Hamburg in 1911, large steel hulled square riggers were still being built. F. Laeisz ran the Flying 'P' Line and its giant sailing ships became legendary. To name but a few, the following five are good examples - *Pamir*, *Passat*, *Peking*, *Potosi* and *Preussen*. The *Peking*, a 3,120 grt barque was chosen in 1932 as a replacement for the old 'static' training ship *Arethusa*, on the Thames. Renamed by the 'Shaftesbury Homes and Arethusa Training Ship', the ex *Peking* was duly moored at Upnor and would serve for the next forty two years, specialising in seamanship skills necessary for large numbers of boys intending to make a career at sea. In 1975 the ship finally went out of use and despite local ideas for preservation, she was auctioned and duly crossed the Atlantic to South Street Seaport Museum, New York. By the time of this image she had already lost her topgallant masts, yet still looks very impressive. The Everard owned coastal sailing barge *Cambria* 79r/1906 also traded under sail alone, last of her type so to do, when retired from trade in 1967. The Upnor view shows her still in trading condition. Later, she would move to the then, fledgling Sailing Barge Museum at Sittingbourne.

31. SS GLEN STRATHALLAN

Built by Cochranes of Selby, Yorkshire, this 330 gross ton steamer dated from 1928, and was launched as a private yacht for Mr R.A. Cubbin of Douglas, Isle of Man. In 1954 she was offered to the Shaftesbury Homes and duly lay alongside *Arethusa* at Upnor for some time as a 'steamship' class room. In 1960, the King Edward VII Nautical College in London chartered her to act as a seagoing training ship for navigating officers. As such, many of us remember fondly the odd trip down to the Thames Estuary from the Millwall Docks base in the 1960s. By 1970 the old ship needed costly work - she was not broken up but unusually, 'scuttled' off Plymouth-thereby continuing her training role, but this time for divers!

Map No.4   Medway Estuary

(1)   Kingsnorth Jetty
(2)   Otterham Creek and Quay
(3)   Halstow Creek
(4)   Site of Isle of Grain-BP Refinery Thamesport Container Terminal
(5)   Port Victoria

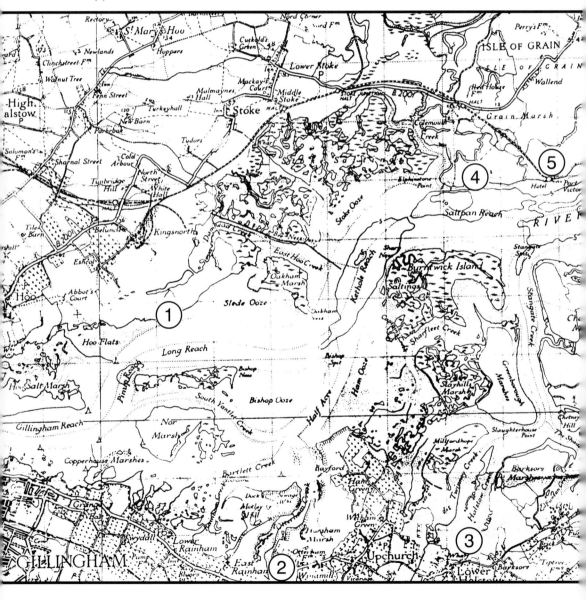

32. STORMY PETREL

A timeless scene in Gillingham Reach in 2005 with countryside beyond, and the recently restored fishing smack 71FM, *Stormy Petrel* lies quietly at her mooring. She was built at Whitstable in 1890, and has never been motor powered. At 40ft in length she is surely as smart as the day when launched.

33. MV HOLMON at Kingsnorth

The massive chimney of Kingsnorth Power Station has dominated the Lower Medway area for several decades. Originally supplied by the steam colliers and entirely unloaded by grab crane, coal handling today has advanced considerably. Alongside is the Swedish bulk carrier *Holmon* 8,383g/1978. Just astern of the passing yacht can be seen a sophisticated shipboard coal unloader. The after side has a large grab crane arrangement not in use, whilst the forward side has a covered conveyor arm, from which can be seen a steady stream of coal dropping the few feet to the jetty hopper/conveyor system. Coal is drawn from the ship's holds by screw conveyor and thence delivered ashore. Power station coal is traditionally 'small stuff'- almost dusty- and therefore bits do not end up all over decks and hatch covers, or jetty surfaces as was always the case before. The need for shore based cranes and drivers, has also been reduced, although just off to the right, one grab crane can still deal with the unloading of non-geared ships.

34. EDITH MAY at Halstow

The 64r/1906 Harwich built sailing barge *Edith May* is undergoing restoration here in 2005. She is sitting in a purpose built berth and a substantial overall shelter has been constructed to afford weather protection. It is to be hoped that another barge has been saved for the 'active' barge fleet. Locally, Eastwoods Brickworks ran barges such as *Cumberland* 44r/1900, and *Dabchick* 36r/1895. The 42 ton *Durham* sported a curious cut down rig when locally engaged on the mud collection run from nearby Stangate Creek. Loaded by an army of 'shovellers' over the low tide, the mud was a valued ingredient for brickmaking.

35. SIRDAR →

Although out of trade for some years before this 1968 photograph, *Sirdar* 53r/1898 and built at Ipswich, was in splendid form. She had switched to the more genteel 'hospitality' industry, as evidenced by the partial conversion of her cargo hold to accommodation. When in trade she last operated for London & Rochester. The photograph catches her 'gliding' past the Isle of Grain jetties, bound for the Thames Estuary.

36. SS KENT →

It may seem strange to include this ocean going steam tanker here, but her name, local and personal connections, seem so to warrant. *Kent* 31,763grt/1960 and her sister ship *Derby*, were built to the order of Federal Tankers Ltd. At around this period, each individual P & O constituent company entered the deep sea tanker market, supplying one to three ships each to the 'Group' fleet. By 1963, some fifteen tankers were brought together under the guise of Trident Tankers Ltd, who then continued fleet expansion for some years. SS *Kent* was chartered out to BP carrying crude oil from the Gulf, Caribbean, West and North Africa to BP refineries around Europe. Visits to the Isle of Grain, 'Kent' Refinery were not uncommon. In the 1960 photograph the ship is obviously new, but it would not be too long before a change of hull colour better suited to the trade, would occur. This ship however always retained her 'Federal' funnel marking - red, black top and white Federal flag. Sold in 1968, at 48,873dwt tons this was a large crude oil tanker of the day - soon all new oil tankers would be built to the current 'all-aft' design.

37. MTs SERVICEMAN and IRISHMAN

That familiar shape of Kingsnorth Power Station looms in the distance in this 1968 scene. Lying alongside SS *Kent* are two units of Hull based United Towing's tug fleet. The older, outboard tug *Serviceman* 330g/1945 and converted from steam to motor in 1961, can muster 2000BHP. Inboard lies her more modern sister ship *Irishman* 450g/1966, and of 5000BHP. The two tugs had delivered an ailing SS *Kent* to the Isle of Grain, following a serious breakdown out in the Atlantic a few days earlier. Note *Irishman* sports a shamrock painted on the bulkhead.

38. Departing Grain

Cargo discharged and ship ballasted, the journey under tow to Falmouth Drydock for repairs commences with Irishman at the bow. Two days of onboard preparations for drydocking then followed for arrival at Falmouth. In more general terms the scene epitomises BP Grain at this period – tankers are working cargo almost continuously at every berth. The BP ship just ahead is of the then, 'newer' all aft construction.

39. Thamesport Container Terminal

So enormous and continuous have industrial changes been on the Isle of Grain, that a brief timescale of events follows: The Medway's deepwater hereabouts has always been the catalyst for development. In 1923 oil storage facilities were established, and by 1948 work began on the BP Kent refinery, which fully opened in 1955. Gradually more jetties for crude and clean oils came into service as the plant expanded. Crude oil imports, however ceased in around 1982 leaving a product storage facility, and by 1985 only a few jetties were in use. 1998 saw a large scale stone/aggregate importing and handling facility open, and subsequently much remote construction work for the Channel Tunnel project took place here, making full use of Grain's rail link. Since this time, a major part of the upriver end of the site has been developed as an international container handling port. This is capable of accepting the largest container ships, and the smaller 'feeder' ships, necessary to that trade. The latest development is the construction of a brand new LNG importing terminal and special berth for this type of tanker. Strangely, this particular site is where the largest crude oil ships once docked in the 1970s, and earlier still had been the location of Port Victoria. In this 2005 scene, Hapag Lloyds' *Essen Express* 53,815g/1993 lies under four of the container gantries. Ahead of her is the 3,994g/1995 built German 'feeder' vessel, *Jacob Becker*.

40. Port Victoria (Isle of Grain) 1905

In 1883 the South Eastern Railway built their branch line onto the Isle of Grain terminating on a newly constructed 400ft long wooden pier, protruding into the Medway. Port Victoria had arrived. The enterprise would connect with the steam packets running to the Continent. The venture, on the face of it, appears almost to have been one of 'spite' since the rival London, Chatham & Dover Railway had a perfectly viable and less remote operation across the Medway at Queenborough Pier. This had been up and running since 1860. In 1883 a gale wrecked Port Victoria Pier, but it was duly reinstated. Between 1900 and 1904 the night ferry to Flushing moved across to Port Victoria from Queenborough - its pier caught fire and burned down- for the second time. However, Port Victoria's fortunes never improved and eventually the pier and railway station, in some terminal decay, closed in 1951, only to be swallowed-up in the subsequent BP Refinery development. The 1905 photograph shows tank engine and branch line train with crew posing for the camera. A long way from the exotic boat trains once probably dreamed of by the line's forebears. Far left, a single spare coach awaits traffic that never materialised, and this really is one forgotten Continental link.

41. The new LNG Terminal in 2005 →

Seen complete and awaiting its first shipment, the new gas import terminal stands roughly where Port Victoria bravely faced the future, one hundred years earlier. The large concrete chimney off to the right is that of Grain's oil fired power station.

42. Sheerness Docks →

Upon closure of the Royal Naval Dockyard in 1960, Sheerness made the transition to modern commercial port. Historically, the Navy had been around since 1600 with major local expansion in the 1800s. In its new role deepwater berths have been created for ocean going ships in the timber, refrigerated cargo, container and car handling trades, plus berths for roll-on, roll-off traffic. In the 1970s steelmaking became a growth industry, often utilising scrap metal from ships dismantled nearby. In 1975, the Olau Line started their roll-on, roll-off freight and passenger service to Flushing. 1980 saw the start of a 'Baco-liner', (barge carrying ship), service to West Africa, calling also at Bremen and Flushing. 15,000 ton ferries were brought onto the Flushing route

in 1980 and such was their success that by 1990, two 33,000 ton ships *Olau Britannia* and *Olau Hollandia* appeared. In common with other ports, once the Channel Tunnel opened, local ferry traffic dwindled and Olau Line duly departed, leaving Eurolink to maintain a freight service, until closure of the route in 1997. In this 2005 photograph from left to right we see the Swedish vehicle ferry *Eva Oden* 16,948g/1979, the coaster *Cemluna* 2,705g/1991 and Cool Carriers refrigerated cargo ship *Summer Bay* 12,260g/1979 - a traditional 'reefer' of a design not to be seen for much longer.

← 43. MT KEVERNE off Garrison Point

The familiar outline of Garrison Point has welcomed generations of seafarers, Royal and Merchant into the Medway. The Port Authority's control radar can be seen perched atop, whilst J.P. Knight's MT *Keverne* 260g/1960 and built with a special fire-fighting platform for use at BP Grain, assists the United Towing tug at the bow of SS *Kent*. A small coaster waits ahead for a clear channel inwards, in this 1968 view.

← 44. Garrison Point in 2005

The Medway Ports Authority tower has risen in order to 'peer' over the ex Flushing Terminal which had been constructed to seaward for the larger ferries. This berth is just visible beyond the tugs mooring. Two powerful modern tugs await their next job, *Lady Sarah* 370g/1991 and *Adsteam Victory* 495g/2000. Tug shapes, power and propulsion systems have changed much in recent years and these two have all-round visibility wheelhouses, and are also fitted as fire-fighters.

45. ex. MV OLAU BRITANNIA

As if to emphasize the shifting patterns of ferry operation in recent years, here we see the old *Olau Britannia* in her next guise as *Pride of Portsmouth* 33,336g/1989. Together with the ex. *Olau Hollandia* (*Pride of Le Havre*), P & O took the ships on for their Portsmouth to Le Havre route. This ceased operating towards the end of 2005. The Channel Tunnel effect, the cessation of much 'duty-free' traffic, and fierce competition from the low cost airline front, all impinge on successful cross-Channel ferry operations.

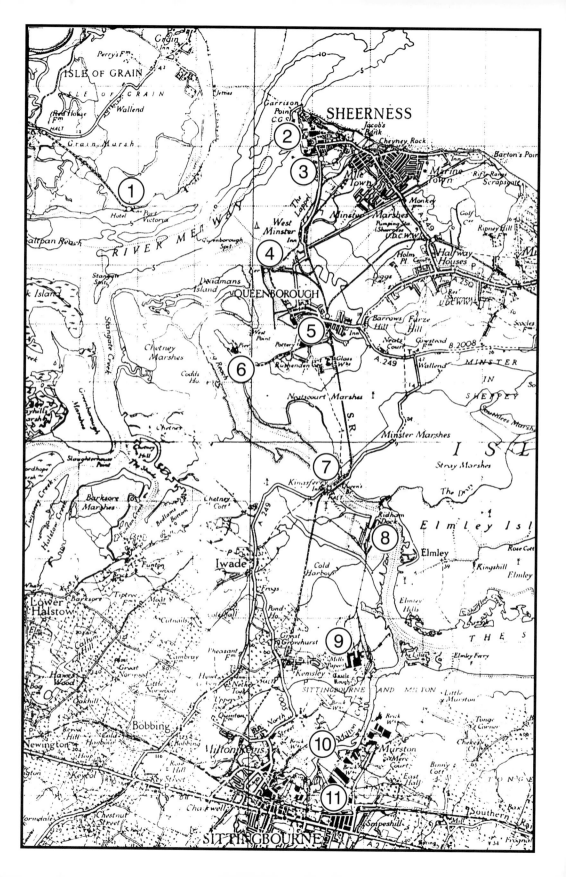

← Map No.5 Sheerness and The Swale

46. SS SAN DARIO

The well known old Eagle Oil and Shipping Company were early operators of ocean going steam tankers between the Wars. Ultimately, in the 1950s, their large fleet merged with that of Shell. Here in the post WWII years we see *San Dario* 1,137g/1918, a veteran coastal steam tanker. She has just discharged somewhere locally and heads off for another cargo, probably bunker oil. Her shore hose connection can be seen permanently slung from the derrick. Nearing the end of a long working life when photographed here, the clean white upperworks nevertheless show that someone cared.

47. MV NINA BOWATER

The Bowater Steamship Company built up their own fleet of ships to serve their specific cargo requirements. In this 1960s view, *Nina Bowater* 4,017g/1961 and one of several similar, was designed to bring woodpulp for the paper mills and take away finished paper for export. Although plainly suited for other general cargo, this class of ship was particularly deep draughted for their Swale restricted overall length. Hulls were painted green and the Bowater emblem can be seen on the funnel.

48. MV LORD CITRINE

Until the 1960s coastal colliers rarely exceeded 4,600 tons dwt, suited to most of the lower Thames, and other power station berths. Also they largely remained an 'enclave' of steam power, long after most types had switched to motor propulsion. As London's riverside power stations were phased out, new larger generating stations came into service downstream, in deeper water areas. *Lord Citrine* 14,200g/1986 and 22,000 dwt, illustrates this development. In the 1980s photograph the ship appears new and is carrying the 'Powergen' logo on her funnel. She is still however totally reliant on shore grab crane discharge.

49. Queenborough Creek →

Now largely serving as a fishing and small boat haven, the Creek can be closed off in the event of forecasted storm, sea surge or exceptionally high tide. A flood barrier was installed here in 1983 when considerable works of a similar nature took place along the North Kent Coast shoreline.

50.   Queenborough waterfront in 2005 →

Passing by en route to the sea is the Dutch motor coaster *Daniel* 1,999g/1996. She had earlier left a wharf higher up the Swale beyond Ridham Dock. Fifty years ago Dutch coasters ranged typically from 200 to 500 gross tons, and could lift from 250 to 1,000 tons of cargo. *Daniel* can manage around 3,000 tons. Off to the right of this view once stood Queenborough Railway Pier, already mentioned, with its station for the Flushing steamer service of the 1860s onward. The Pier closed as early as 1916 and yet apart from use in two World Wars the infrastructure remained mostly intact until demolition in the 1950s. The Flushing night boat service moved to Folkestone in 1911, leaving the day boat to soldier on for a while, before Zeeland Shipping decided to clear out of Kent completely in 1926. Thereafter they concentrated all services at Harwich, Essex. In 1930 Philip Speakman joined forces with John Settle thus forming Settle, Speakman and Co. Ltd. Their early ventures had been in local coal handling, chalk and cement industries. Beyond the *Daniel*, can be seen the landmark cranes of Washer Wharf, a site much used for chalk, coal, steel and scrap metal handling. By 1972 Shipbreaking Queenborough Ltd were dismantling ships for scrap to supply the local steel mills. In the early 1990s Queenborough Rolling Mills were in production, and Klondike Wharf, nearby, handled fertiliser cargoes.

51. Kingsferry Bridge (1904)

Shipping heading up the Swale to Ridham Dock from Queenborough must pass through Kingsferry Bridge - Sheppey's only road and rail access point to mainland Kent. In 1860, the Sittingbourne and Sheerness Railway Company drove their new line across the Swale, thus eliminating an ancient ferry. The first bridge was deemed insufficient as trains grew heavier so, in 1904 this 'lift and roll' type structure came into service with single railtrack and roadway combined. This is the bridge seen here in the 1958 photograph with an old cargo steamer passing through. At the bow, is one of Gaselee's, London tugs. A firm more usually associated with Thames lighterage work, they nevertheless had a towage contract for shipping on the Swale.

52. Kingsferry Bridges (1960 and 2006) →

This 2005 view along the bank of the Swale shows the branch train trundling towards Sheerness, on the Isle of Sheppey. It has just crossed the central, vertically lifting bridge section between the high concrete support towers. The structure dates from 1960 when it replaced that shown in No.51. Huge recent increases in road usage, especially that of heavy goods vehicles, plus serious and frequent delays to permit the passage of shipping, have necessitated construction of yet another new bridge. The latest version is seen here taking shape as a graceful arc. It is to be a high level roadway meaning traffic flow will not be stopped for shipping to and from Ridham Dock. In the far distance, the Isle of Grain Power Station chimney makes a good landmark.

53. Ridham Dock →

Newspaper owner Edward Lloyd wanted better transport links for his substantial paper empire's raw material handling and manufacturing process. The Sittingbourne site, established in 1877 suffered from the shallow nature of the Creek itself. In 1913 work began to excavate a new deep water dock on the banks of the Swale, just above Kingsferry Bridge. This would permit the use of much larger ships for his cargoes. WWI intervened and the Military took over the Dock for the duration, not handing it back for civilian use until 1921. In 1924, the large Kemsley Paper Mills opened around halfway between Ridham Dock and Sittingbourne. Materials were transported by a narrow gauge industrial steam railway and an aerial ropeway system. In fact the Sittingbourne end of the tramway began as a horse drawn entity before conversion to steam power in 1906. Edward Lloyd

continued to own the mills until 1948 when the Bowater era began. In the 1950s china clay for the paper making process was shipped into Ridham Dock thence barged up to Kemsley; later the commodity would arrive from Cornwall direct by rail. Barges would be back-loaded with export paper for the waiting steamers at Ridham, or Queenborough buoys. As we have already seen, ships up to around 5,000 tons capacity can reach Ridham on the tide. Bowater Lloyd Pulp & Paper Mills owned one small tug of their own, the *Elizabeth Murre* 46g/1930. The 1930s photograph shows the Dock devoid of steamers, but a number of well tarpaulined, laden lighters are in evidence, along with the ever present sprit sail barges.

54. MVs LOVISA GORTHON and IVAN GORTHON

The Swedish, Gorthon Company specialised in ships well suited to the timber and paper trades. Here, around 1960, we see two units of their fleet berthed in Ridham Dock. The nearest vessel is *Lovisa Gorthon* 2,112g/1953. Beyond lies *Ivan Gorthon* 1,967g/1955, and to all intents and purposes an identical sister ship. The 1955 version does have the newer design bi-pod mast arrangement, but differs little otherwise.

55. Ridham Dock in 2005 →

A view across the Dock shows a more modern group of cranes to serve the ships. Barely visible is the bridge structure of the 'low-level' motor coaster *Waltzberg* 1,961g/1991 and already on her fourth name. With a gross tonnage much the same as the earlier Gorthon ships, the profile could hardly be more different.

56. Swale Wharf, Kemsley →

Already seen passing Queenborough (No.50), the Dutchman *Daniel* is just completing unloading at this remote wharf, near Kemsley Mills. Coasters working at such places are becoming something of a rarity in general, around the country today.

57. P.A.M. at Milton Creek

This is industrial Sittingbourne at its height in the 1900s with sailing barges, steam cranes and even a steam tug present. The barge 'bow on' to the right is Wakely Bothers *P.A.M.* 50r/1901 and built at Rochester. She has particularly ornate gold scroll-work on the bow. The shallow nature of the Creek here dictated a twice daily period of activity, as soon as the tide rose sufficiently. Even so, it was not 'all work and no play'- a couple of recreational craft are visible- including one with a lugsail.

58. PIONEER (barge) at Sittingbourne →

The nearest barge is Edward Lloyd's *Pioneer* 66r/1898 and built not far away at Teynham. She has largely been de-rigged for local use and yet still retains her leeboards. A steam grab crane is unloading coal from a steel Thames lighter. Rolls of finished newsprint await loading on the quayside. This particular image really does emphasize the creek's dependency on shallow draughted vessels.

59. HISTED at Adelaide Dock, Murston →

In 1850 Smeed, Dean & Co Ltd were heavily into brickmaking, lime and cement manufacturing. By 1877 as we have seen, Sittingbourne had its Edward Lloyd paper mill. To these industries must be added the barge building exploits of Charles Burley, Wills & Packham, White, and Shrubshall. Some examples are:- *Charles Burley* 52r/1902, *Bankside* 60r/1900, *Youngarth* 63r/1913, *Persevere* 58r/1899. Smeed took the shallow draught hull type to its ultimate - much larger craft, but with more conventional rig. *Emily Smeed*, 272g/1872 was just one such vessel. Rigged as a barquentine with leeboards, she was able to carry 500 tons instead of the customary 100 to 150 tons per barge hull. The hybrid design was quite successful but reportedly difficult to sail to windward. The Murston area soon grew pockmarked with clay pits as the brick industry expanded - the growth of London being the main consumer. Adelaide Dock became well known for the loading of the 'brickie' barges, and the 1930s photograph shows hand loading of bricks into the after end of *Histed's* hold. This 53r/1880 barge belonged to Smeed, Deans' fleet and had originally sailed under the name of *Lydia*. A barge could carry 40-45,000 bricks and the capped lads here are loading six at a time with bare hands and arms. Tough lot, indeed - one can only ponder the degree of back-ache at the end of each working day!

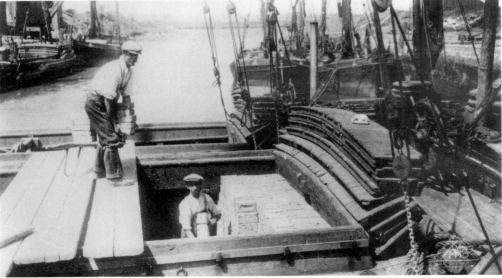

← 60. CELTIC

Once a member of E.J.&W. Goldsmiths' large fleet, *Celtic* 120r/1903, was nicknamed an 'ironpot' although steel hulled. This term mainly differentiated the fewer steel barges from the masses of wooden hulls about. She came from a Dutch yard at Papendrecht along with others, each capable of carrying around 230 tons of cargo. In 1941 *Celtic* was motorised and given twin screw propulsion, thus forsaking all traces of sail. After WWII she ran in the bagged cement trade from Asham Cement Works, on the River Ouse in Sussex and about five miles inland, to Newport, Isle of Wight. This trade lasted until 1967 when the works closed and cargoes were then loaded at Shoreham or Greenhithe. By 1969, the old barge was laid up at Newport and owner Alf Sheaf replaced her with the ex- Dutch coaster *Dina* 198g/1939, renamed *Ash Lake*. After a while *Celtic* worked in the Thames area, before moving to Sittingbourne where some restoration work took place. Alas, at the end of 2005 the Dolphin Sailing Barge Museum closed. This had been Charles Burley's barge yard.

61. CAMBRIA and OAK

Already seen in her full regalia (No.30), here *Cambria* is under restoration by the Cambria Trust at Sittingbourne. A frame has been erected to give some weather protection whilst work progresses. The Trust has much to do to preserve this famous old wooden hulled Everard barge from 1906. Just visible to the right is the bow and hand windlass of the Maldon built barge *Oak* 43r/1881, a smaller type, now too awaiting better times.

62. Conyer Creek (right)

Conyer Creek saw its fair share of barge activity with nearby Eastwoods Brickworks, and barge construction by White. Some examples were *Alpha* 42r/1897, *Annie Byford* 54r/1914, *Charles Hutson* 56r/1899, *Durham* 42r/1899, *Joy* 56r/1914 and *Westmoreland* 43r/1900. The actual recorded build place was sometimes referred to hereabouts as nearby Teynham, to which Conyer adjoins. In the 2005 photograph some waterside redevelopment has occurred, and since sailing barge hulls suitable as houseboats are in short supply, an influx of Dutch barge types is ongoing. These craft have crossed the North Sea having been made redundant in their own country, to fill the gap. In this scene at least two ex 'Luxemotor' types are visible having made the conversion. The nearest craft, devoid of all gear, is an ex 'Tjalk' type, not dissimilar to our sailing barges, and once a carrier of leeboards, too.

**Map No.6
The Swale,
Conyer to
Faversham**

(1) Conyer Creek
(2) Oare Creek
(3) Faversham Creek

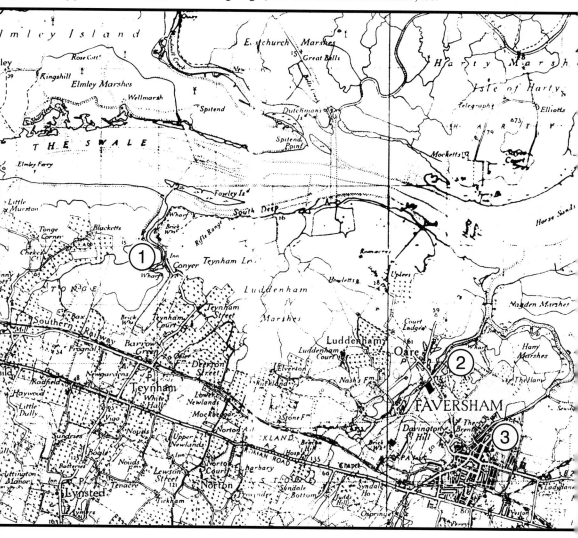

(centre picture)
63. PERSEVERE

Such has been the attraction of living afloat that a good many long serving, ex- commercial barge types have made the transition at the end of their working days. Here, two massive 'swim-headed' steel lighters have been so converted. To the left is the *Persevere* 58r/1889 and Murston built. She last traded as a fully powered motor barge and had run for the Associated Portland Cement Manufacturers fleet. The fact that any wooden hulled craft can survive 116 years is a wonderful testament to builders, materials used and owners down the years, considering the punishing and abrasive nature of their environment.

(lower left)
64. Oare Creek powder barges

Remote Oare Creek must have seemed a safe choice for the export of locally manufactured gunpowder. Horse drawn tramway trucks and covered wagons certainly shouldn't generate unwanted sparks! In this 1920s scene two shirt-sleeved gents appear to be keeping a close eye and tally on the proceedings. The three barges visible could shift well over three hundred tons between them—individually small craft, but they most definitely had numbers on their side.

65. GWYNRONALD

East Greenwich built this 85r/1908 barge would have traded further afield well beyond the Thames Estuary for her owner Samuel West & Co. Ltd. They ran a very large fleet for decades, and were most successful at picking up whatever cargo was on offer along the way. Still in possession of her lower mast, she now sits in a mud berth, partially the key to survival for old wooden hulls, surrounded by modern yachts.

Faversham

For centuries this has been a port of some significance despite the relatively shallow access creek. By the 1890s some 500,000 tons of cargo were handled annually, by up to twenty five ship movements per day. Grain, timber, bricks, fertiliser, explosives, and coal (domestic, industrial and gasworks), were typical cargoes. In 1875 J. Pollock's Shipyard started turning out many types of small ship and would so continue until their 1970 closure. Another well known shipbuilder and owner was Goldfinch. Many sailing ships other than barges were owned or registered in the port, ie Brigs, Ketches and Schooners. Even some of the popular Prince Edward Island Barquentines were Faversham registered, such as:- *Joseph* 1879, *Carmenta* 1875, and *LC Owen* of 1878. The Whitstable built schooner *Zebrina* 142r/1873 was similarly registered. In the 1950s BP had their own clean oil distribution depot opposite the Shipyard, served directly by esturial tanker from the refinery. By the 1980s small ships were feeling the pinch from two directions, firstly road transport, and secondly from larger vessels - physically unable to enter such havens as Faversham. Today the port houses Kent's 'active' sailing barge fleet, so tall masts and sprits still grace the creek. Some examples of Pollock built ships follow:- *Arran Monarch* 147g/1946, *Ballyedward* 552g/1950 (ex *Goldlynx*), *BP Haulier* 315g/1955, *Camroux I,II & III* 324g/404g/1935, *Dominence* 263g/1940, *Ferrocrete* 158g/1927, *Empire Creek* 332g/1941, *Lady Sophia* 226g/1938 and *Stourgate* 115g/1924.

66. Brigs at Faversham

This delightfully busy scene in the 1890s is reproduced from a glass slide original that has been hand tinted. Two old brigs, with their yards 'cock-billed' out of the way of passing traffic, are at the timber yard wharf, just below the swingbridge. The Commissioners' steam paddle tug, (see No.69), lies nearby in original livery. *Pioneer*, 60g/1883, was iron hulled and could muster 40 NHP. She was built for 'The Commissioners for the Navigation, Faversham'.

67. SUNBEAM (schooner)

In the foreground in this 1900s view is the two masted top-sail schooner *Sunbeam* 93r/1860, built at Hartlepool and registered at Faversham. Beyond her lies a large ketch and elsewhere familiar 'sprits' abound. *Sunbeam* is discharging by boom and gin, in the time honoured way, the gear being clearly visible between fore and mainmast.

68. Towards the swingbridge

A number of Edwardian folk cross the distant swingbridge, the shipping access to the upper harbour basin, whilst others parade along the footpath. A couple of sailing barges over at the wharf appear ready for action, whatever it might be. Far right, *Pioneer's* distinctive funnel shows up through the trees.

69. PT PIONEER
In this 1900s scene the Commissioners have brought their 'pride and joy' paddle tug somewhat up to date with what now would be termed 'a makeover'. Gone are the black funnel and hull. Motor tyres were not yet plentiful enough to become instant tug fenders. Along the commercial quays the expected sailing barges are busy working cargo at the warehouses. Compare this scene to No.74, taken from the swingbridge in 2005.

70. Passing through the swingbridge
An unidentifiable barge 'ghosts' through to the upper harbour, whilst other craft are moored at the timber wharf. This image, also from the 1890s, is the second from a glass slide, hand coloured original - see No.66.

71. GOLDFINCH

J.M. Goldfinch built this unusual 'schooner-barge' here in Faversham 117r/1894. She had a typical ketch-barge style shallow hull and leeboards, yet was rigged in the manner of a double top-sail schooner. The image is a rare one as it shows the ship in original condition in Camperdown Dock, Dundee around 1900. Later she was cut down to ketch rig, still with top sails, and in 1930 went across the Atlantic with other redundant ketches, for service in British Guiana.

← 72. MV LADY SOPHIA

Completed in 1938 by J. Pollock & Son, Faversham for Thomas Watson Shipping of Rochester, here we see the 286g/280dwt *Lady Sophia*. Craft of this type were increasingly attracting the attention of British owners - partly in response to an 'invasion' of efficient little Dutch motor coasters. Watsons ran a number of similar sized ships at the time, but this example went to Danish owners as *Sjoholm* in 1957. Beyond *Lady Sophia* another hull up on the slipway is nearing launch readiness.

73. MT BP HAULIER

Designed for service under the Thames bridges, the low superstructure of *BP Haulier* would be vital. The other criteria for such craft - a shallow draught would permit access to such oil depots as Faversham. Ships had of necessity to be launched sideways here due to lack of waterway width. As is the custom at launches, flags aplenty are flying and the photographer in the foreground will have to be alert for the 'backwash'! Pollocks launched this 315 grt "oil barge for river and esturial service" in August 1955.

74. Faversham Quays, 2005

This image should be viewed in conjunction with No.69, downstream from the swingbridge. New apartments here have replaced commercial activity and the creek has narrowed somewhat as plant growth consolidates siltation. In the distance, new homes occupy the site of the former shipyard, yet one old warehouse roofline can still be detected, having mercifully been incorporated into the general design of things.

75. The 'active' barge fleet

Further downstream in 2005 on the East bank, a number of active restored barges are now based. Truncated modern steel lighters have been pressed into service to make mini floating docks for the underwater upkeep of old hulls. Apart from one modern Dutch 'Luxemotor' type, the barges visible here are, from left to right:

Decima 67r/1899, *Greta* 46r/1892, *Henry* 44r/1904, *Lady of the Lea* 1931, and *Repertor* 69r/1924.

76. Towards Faversham →

Looking upstream towards the Town, this creekside view shows a variety of moored craft. The ketch rigged vessel is *Bella of Bow*, an ex Dutch auxiliary type. Alongside her with gear lowered is the sailing barge *Orinoco* 70r/1895, she once belonged to Cranfield Brothers of Ipswich. Beneath a white cover close to the old United Fertiliser building, *Ironsides* 78r/1900 awaits restoration.

Map No. 7   Whitstable and Herne Bay

(1)   Whitstable Harbour   (2)   Herne Bay and Neptunes Arm

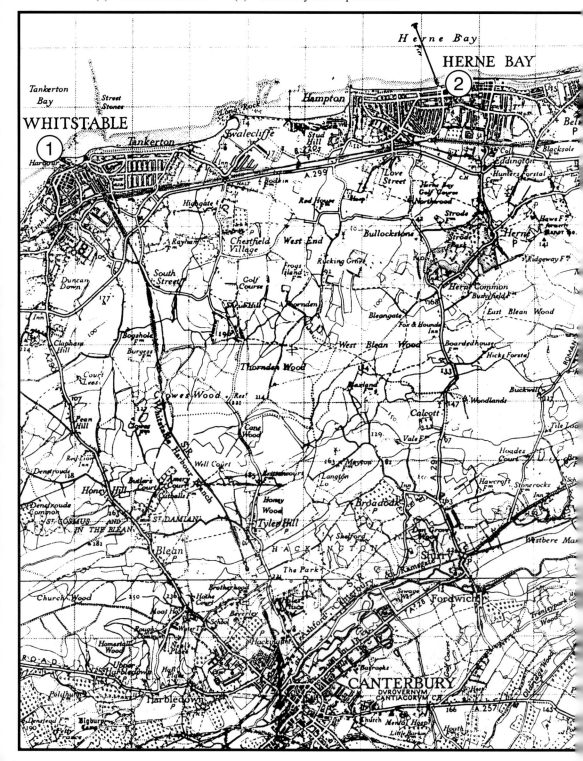

Whitstable

North Kent had a reputation for oysters in abundance from Roman times onward, however, it is only in the last century that the 'edible succulent bi-valve' has achieved exclusive status. For centuries it had been thought of as food for the masses, and deemed almost a staple diet amongst common folk. The seabed growing and harvesting of this commodity has had such an effect on Whitstable's economy and maritime activity, that it simply cannot be omitted, at least with regard to its carriage to market by hoy.

The town's proximity to Canterbury has similarly ensured much commerce for the port. In 1830 the Canterbury and Whitstable Railway arrived, enabling direct goods transfer from the ships in the harbour by 1832. By 1836 a steamer, the *William the Fourth*, began running to London on alternate days for the Canterbury and Whitstable Steam Packet Company. Direct rail communication arrived in 1860. In the late 1800s, a number of local shipowners merged to form the Whitstable Shipping Company, and local ship building was quite prolific.

By the 1900s, coal arrived by steam coaster increasingly as the last of the old brigantines lost favour. Some examples of ships locally built: *Zebrina* 142r/1873 a schooner, *Azima* 50r/1878 a sailing barge and similar, *Northdown* 86r/1924. Daniels Brothers ran this latter craft, and indeed were still running barges in the 1950s. The flow of coal reversed in the 1930s as Chislet Colliery exported, but in 1952 the goods only railway to Canterbury closed.

The 1960s saw the London and Rochester Company open a special direct general cargo service to Esbjerg, Denmark. Whitstable has always attracted the smaller Thames Estuary type traders, as their 'smooth water' limit extended thus far. In the 1980s Baltic timber, grain and aggregates were being handled by ships up to around 2,000 tons carrying capacity, as indeed is the case today.

77. GOOD INTENT

Sitting on the beach off Whitstable probably in the 1880s is the hoy *Good Intent* 66r/1844, locally built and Faversham registered. Classed simply as a 'smack', by 1882 when she was owned by Mr John Collard of Herne Bay, the type is a very old one indeed, and the photograph although indistinct is a rare survivor. It shows a heavily constructed deep vessel, with long bowsprit and excessively long booms of the old hoy type. A light boom and gin tackle can be seen rigged for cargo handling and shortly, horses, carts and carters will make good use of the lack of water. By this time the days of the passenger carrying hoys were well over, but many soldiered on, carrying any cargo offered. In the 1850s, some fourteen local hoys were carrying oysters to London, in one hundred bushel batches.

78. RAVEN and DOLLY VARDEN

Not a steamer in sight in this 1900s photograph, with brigantines rigged to unload at the harbour entrance. On the left is *Raven* 177r/1873 and one of the Prince Edward Island built ships. The *Dolly Varden*, 186r/1871, came from a yard at Bideford, North Devon, from where many shipwrights would depart, taking their skills to such places as Prince Edward Island, where good, cheap and plentiful timber still abounded.

79. SERVIC at Whitstable →

The sailing barge nearest the camera here in 1910 with the long pole boom is the *Servic* 162g/1904. Dutch built, she was one of the Celtic's sister barges, and originally part of E.J.&W.Goldsmith's fleet. This example was motorised quite early in her career in 1933 with a 100HP engine. Also in unloading action are a couple of brigantines and far right the distinctive stern board of another sailing barge.

80. MBs SERVIC and NICOLA DAWN →

This image dates from the mid 1950s. Amazingly the now fully motorised *Servic* is lying in the same berth as forty years previously (No.79). Her sailing rig has been totally eliminated in deference to motor propulsion and a small foremast and derrick have been installed. On the opposite quayside at the grain elevator two more 'esturial' traders are moored. The inner craft is *Nicola Dawn* 137g/1955 and a purpose built sailing barge replacement type. Both these ships were operated by the London & Rochester Company at the time. Amongst the pleasure craft visible, the now ubiquitous 'plastic' hulls of today had yet to displace traditional wooden construction. (Copyright, The Francis Frith Collection,SP3 5QP).

81. MV TRIUMPH

With the Seasalter and Ham Oyster Fishery Company shed beyond, the Dutch coaster *Triumph* 386g/1961 has her derricks swung out of the way to allow shore crane operation. The trend to shore cranes would lead to the virtual absence of shipboard derricks on most coastal vessels. However, today there is a partial reverse here, as some owners have started fitting hydraulic cranes adapted from shore based applications to their ships. These are normally centrally mounted, long-arm hydraulic types, suited for bulk cargo discharge by grab.

82. MV RESURGENCE →

In 1958 the local firm of Daniels Brothers was acquired by the London & Rochester Company, and there followed some revival in Whitstable's trading fortunes. The weekly cargo service to Esbjerg was augmented in 1962 when the ex- Swedish cargo ship *Singorita* 552g/1958 joined the run. In the aerial photograph she has been renamed in the Company's traditional coaster naming scheme - *Resurgence*, and clearly exhibits the 'crescent' funnel logo. To distinguish the ship from the reddish brown hulls of the rest of the fleet, a smart light grey, topside paint has been applied.

83. SPEEDWELL →

Seen moored off Whitstable in 1967 is the smack *Speedwell*, a clipper bowed vessel 52ft loa, and built as a tripper boat in 1908. Later she joined the oyster dredging brigade, and an engine was installed in 1922. In recent decades she has been fully restored as a white hulled ketch rigged yacht, and may still be seen on occasion active on the Sussex coast.

84. Whitstable, inner harbour

Long gone are the smaller local cargo traders, yet the harbour still flourishes with fishing vessels. The name *Speedwell* similarly survives hereabouts as perpetuated on the harbour launch in the foreground. Compare this scene with Nos.79 & 80.

85. The harbour entrance in 2005 →

With the basic harbour configuration little altered, this scene makes an interesting comparison to No.78. The outer, opposite quayside now sees bulk aggregate handling.

86. MV HOO FALCON →

The Lapthorn Company of Hoo have progressed from auxiliary barges in the 1950s to a fleet of varying sized, 'mini-bulkers'. *Hoo Falcon* 1,382g/2,225dwt and dating from 1991, represents the largest class. In this 2005 photograph she is in temporary lay-up outside Whitstable's western breakwater. The big increase in size of individual coaster units is highlighted here, as the continuous search for economy of scale, shows no sign of abating. *Hoo Falcon* is exhibiting a new regulatory requirement for all internationally trading ships - an IMO identity number. This stems from increased piracy, cargo theft and ship fraud, particularly in some Far Eastern and West African areas. (IMO stands for the International Maritime Organisation).

87. MV FITZCARRALDO

Quite what the old time 'seadogs' would have made of this multicoloured vessel, is pure guesswork, but the 'Walk the Plank' Theatre Company's ship *Fitzcarraldo* is certainly different. Originally a Scandinavian ferry named *Bjarkoy*, the 286gross ton ship converted to its 'theatrical' role in 1992, and now visits many ports each year in the entertainment industry. It was Whitstable's turn in 2005.

88. DUCHESS OF YORK →

Seen here bowling along in a good breeze around 1907 is a clipper-bowed tripper boat, with a good number of patrons aboard enjoying their outing. Obviously, not everyone was tempted by the paddle steamer trips, locally. A number of gaff rigged tripper boats operated around the East Kent ports and resorts for the holidaymakers, of course a sudden drop in the wind could seriously extend the occasion!

Herne Bay

Small brigs were bringing North-East coal to the beaches of Herne Bay in the 1800s. The first pier was erected in 1832, but lasted only until 1864. In 1899 a three quarter mile long pier, said to be the country's third longest opened for business, ie, the Victorian trippers. By 1914, coal brought ashore for the town's gasworks switched to rail supply, but timber and building materials continued to be barged ashore. The landing points were near the clock tower and along by William Street, until such operations ceased in the 1930s.

In 1993 large scale coastal defence works were undertaken, including 'Neptunes Arm' breakwater, thereby affording a sheltered small boat area, and slipway for same. Herne Bay had seen major storm damage in 1897 and again in the 1953 North Sea storm surge disaster. Around 2000, a sailing tripper boat, the *Wildfire* began operating, thereby reviving an old traditional recreation.

89. The Beach at Herne Bay

A scene in the 1900s with a gaff sail tripper boat beyond, a deeply laden barge has come ashore to unload in the time honoured way. Great seamanship, skill, weather awareness, local knowledge and a bit of luck would be essential for the operation. Ground tackle and anchor would have been set out for the ultimate 'hauling-off' on completion of unloading, and the barge must avoid sitting upon any timber groynes or submerged posts at all costs. Also, the site must be accessible for horses and carts as the tide retreated. Vast quantities of all manner of goods came ashore for centuries on the country's open beaches, before sheltered harbours and wharves came into being. Prayers no doubt were offered up for calm weather, and amazingly accidents were relatively uncommon. Increases in insurance cover and the unpredictability of such operations finally brought about their demise.

90. Two barges at Herne Bay

This beach scene from the 1930s comes right at the end of the 'beach unloading' story. Two barges have come ashore at high water, one laden with sawn timber and the other with possibly, stone blocks. They now await the falling tide for unloading operations to commence. Skippers and crew would not rest easily until their barges were safely back out in deeper water, and around 200 tons needs shifting here, before that stage can be reached.

91. PS MEDWAY QUEEN

Seen here towards the end of her long operational career, the old paddler looks a little uncharacteristically 'down at heel'. Perhaps it was the end of the season but, nevertheless a fair number of patrons are onboard in this 1960s photograph. See No.23 for the ship's details. Summer season round trips to Southend were the order of the day, and unlike the majority of paddlers, *Medway Queen* never sported a wheelhouse in civilian hands, but did whilst away on military duty in WWII. The strange funnel top frame was a late fitting, enabling the ship to hoist an 'after steaming light' the regulatory fifteen feet higher than the forward one. This would thereby show the ship to exceed 150ft loa.

92. Neptunes Arm

The shore end of the truncated pier forms the western end of the new sheltered area established by the construction of the breakwater in 1993. A broad concrete slipway has been formed at the base of the arm to give small boat launching facilities. Just discernible near the entrance at her mooring is the little sailing tripper boat, *Wildfire* sprit rigged when in action.

Map No.8   Margate to Ramsgate   Map No.8.1   Thanet,

(1) Margate Pier and Jetty
(2) North Foreland Lighthouse
(3) Broadstairs Bay
(4) Ramsgate, Inner Basin

Old Island outline →

Dating from the early 1700s, this shows the old Wantsume
Channel much narrowed, as it is believed to have been
three miles wide in places around the year 1000AD.

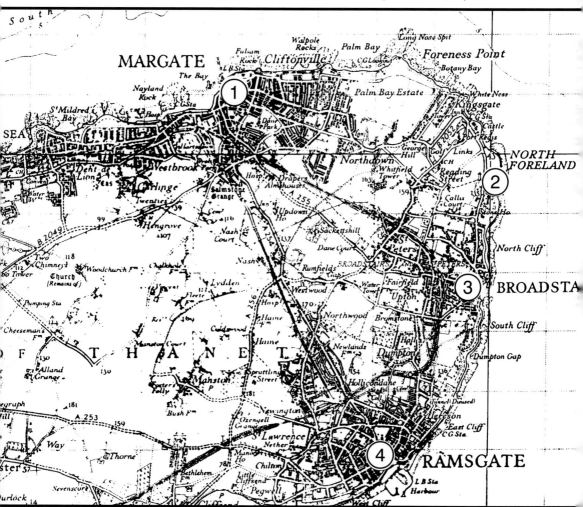

Hoy History

The 'hoy' type is very old indeed having first been mentioned in the late 1400s, carrying grain. They
appear to have been especially popular on the East Coast, Thames and North Kent areas where numbers were
employed 'feeding' London. By nature of their stout construction and seaworthiness, trips out to exposed
anchorages or short passenger voyages were well within their remit. When the country's roads were dangerous
and often impassable, hoys offered a safer, albeit uncomfortable option for travel to the coastal towns.

Typically, in pre-railway days, a journey from London to Margate by hoy in the mid 1700s might take

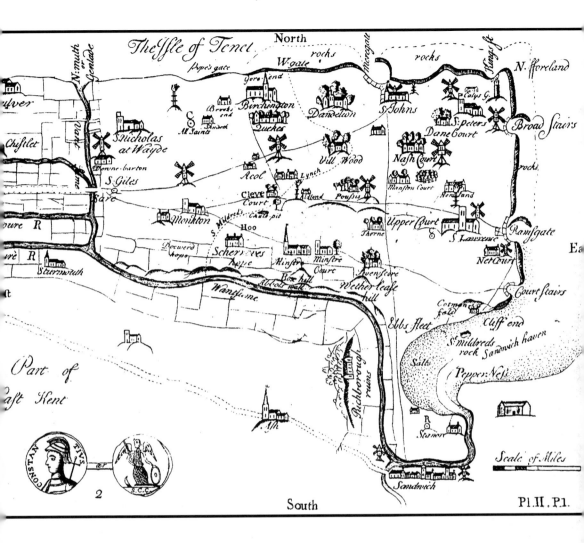

twelve hours or several days, given adverse wind and weather. Onboard conditions were said to be spartan to the point of primitive. The regular hoy services down from the Capital would bring all manner of general goods for local consumption, returning with grain or agricultural produce - or as in the case of Whitstable's hoys - oysters!

The brave souls travelling on these craft must have heaved a sigh of relief when the first paddle steamer smoke appeared over the horizon. This development, together with the arrival of the railways, ended the passenger carrying exploits of the hoys, but many continued for decades carrying freight. The true hoy type seems to have died out before 1900, and locally the shallower, easier to handle sailing barges became their natural successor. Sailing barges on regular runs would still be termed 'hoys' for many more years. The Margate Hoy Company ran the barges *John Bayly*, and *Her Majesty* around 1910. As late as the early 1950s, one motor barge perpetuated the word in her name- *Kentish Hoy*, (ex *Maymom*, ex *Germanic*) of 1904, and yet another of the famous Goldsmith 'ironpots' already described.

By 2000 as we have already seen, small locally generated cargoes had virtually died out - road haulage had won.

93. A model hoy

The photograph, courtesy of the Science Museum London, shows a model hoy from around 1768. It is clearly a bluff, beamy, stoutly constructed vessel with a large hatch abaft the pole mast. A small cabin is located below, right aft. The rig varied somewhat over the centuries but always featured a long bowsprit and very long booms, some carried a square foresail. The model does not feature a sail boom at all. Typically, the craft measured about 60ft loa by 17ft br by 8ft draught, and could carry 80-100 tons of cargo. They would require a larger crew, and the deeper draught made them less handy to operate in comparison to their barge replacements.

Margate

In 1815 John Rennie built the 909ft long 'Whitby' stone pier to replace a wooden one lost in 1808. The year 1817 saw the first steam packet *Thames* arrive after a nine hour trip from London - 'rocket technology' at the time, when compared to the twelve hours to several days, by hoy. By 1827 no less than five steamers belonged to Margate. 1853 saw the building of Margate's iron 'jetty' outwards 1240ft to provide deepwater berths for the steamers. Its hexagonal shaped jetty head could accommodate steamers on the north faces, at any tide state. The structure would suffer from recurring bouts of winter storm damage, over the years.

Famous paddle steamers such as *Koh-I-Noor*, *La Marguerite* and *Royal Sovereign* ran excursions, often to France pre WWI. Later the General Steam Navigation Company ran *Golden Eagle*, *Crested Eagle* and *Royal Eagle*. In 1940, some 46,772 troops ex Dunkirk beaches were landed at Margate.

The stone harbour pier would normally be thronged with sailing barges, fishing boats, steam coasters and latterly, small motor coasters. In 1953 the disastrous North Sea storm surge demolished Rennie's light tower, which was duly replaced by a lesser structure in 1954. In 1958 the last cargo of gasworks coal came ashore and in 1964 the jetty extension head was lost by fire; storms wrecked the remaining structure in 1978.

94. Margate Harbour around 1800 ↗

A delightful line drawing from about this time shows the original light tower beyond a harbour packed with trading vessels, hoys and fishing boats. The following hoys were reportedly trading to Margate in 1804: *Concord, Endeavour, Fortune, Fox, Hero, Industry, King George, Lord Nelson, Mary, New Good Intent, Old Good Intent, Ocean, Old Hero, Queen Providence, Robert & Mary, Union* and *Unity*. As already noted, the Margate Hoy Company still ran sailing barges one hundred years later.

95. SUNBEAM (ketch)

With a steam crane on the pier and the inevitable collection of sailing barges present, well hatted children on the steps await the landing of some monstrous fish. Moored nearby, is the locally built and owned wooden ketch *Sunbeam* 43r/1891. Nearly every coastal town could turn its hand to ship building and Margate was certainly no exception. Photograph dates from the 1920s.

96. Steamers in port

Two ageing little steam coasters are sitting on the bottom in this scene from around 1910, awaiting a rise of tide. One has just about managed to settle within reach of the crane to work cargo. The second is most likely awaiting departure of the first. Depth of water has long been problematical hereabouts - the shallower sailing barges could of course manage to push in a bit further, along the pier.

97. SS QUEENIE and HAWARDEN CASTLE →

The steam coaster *Queenie* 329g/1905 and built at Workington, appears unable to nudge any further in along the quay than the ships in No.96. However, nearer to the camera is the white hulled schooner *Hawarden Castle* 149r/1907. German built at Hammelwerder, she was owned in the 1930s at Connah's Quay, Flintshire and in the photograph looks nearly discharged. Even in this scene, one spritsail barge is visible between the two ships.

98. TSMV QUEEN OF THE CHANNEL →

The New Medway Steam Packet Company had this ship built in 1935 by Denny of Dumbarton. Sadly, she would have but a short life, being lost returning from Dunkirk in May 1940. At 1,162grt, and very up to date in comparison to the Company's paddlers - their 'no wheelhouse' policy was still evidently intact.

99. Margate Pier, distant

Seen departing around 1950 is the *Royal Daffodil* 2,061g/1939 and General Steam Navigation owned. See No.100 for more details.

100. ROYAL DAFFODIL →

The distant subject of No.99 is seen here in close up with a good number of excursion passengers onboard as she slices through a calm sea. At 313ft.loa, 4500 BHP motors gave a speed of 21 knots for the 2073 passengers she was licensed to carry. Summer day trips to France would remain in vogue until the 1960s, when the British public, by and large turned its back on such pursuits, having discovered motoring, flying and the Costa Brava.

101. MV FLUIDITY →

An unusual reason here in 1958 to fly the flags - F.T. Everard's wartime motor coaster *Fluidity* 410g/1944, and once named *Empire Fane*, has just delivered the last seaborne cargo of gasworks coal to Margate. This strange looking little ship was one of nine similarly converted from 'CHANT' –Channel Tankers, to dry cargo mode, by Everards at the end of WWII. Dozens of these ships were built during the War and several owners converted some to cargo ships, whilst many continued to operate in peace time as coastal tankers. Virtually no curved steel plates were used during their construction enabling prefabrication by less experienced firms in wartime. *Fluidity* was 'put together' at Goole in Yorkshire.

102. Margate Harbour, 2005

Sand appears to be progressively taking over now that commercial craft are long gone. In this view, a few small boats look rather forlorn. The 1954 replacement light tower has but little to warn off. See No.96 for earlier view.

103. MB SUCCESS →

A well known trader in the area, this example was motorised in 1932 from her original sailing barge rig. She, too, had begun trading as one of the E.J.&W.Goldsmith's fleet of 'ironpots' as *Cymric* 169r/1903, Dutch built. As a new vessel, rocks on the 'Back of the Wight' interrupted her voyage, but unusually for the time and location, she survived the ordeal. The owners were so delighted they quickly renamed her, *Success*, and indeed she was for decades, finally trading for the London and Rochester Company until the 1960s.

104. MV HOOCREEK (1) →

With a part load of baled waste paper on deck, a regular cargo in the 1950s, the ex Dutch coaster, *Hoocreek* 209g/1928 had joined the growing Lapthorn Company fleet. The firm started with barges in the ballast trade and made their subsequent base at Hoo St.Werburgh, on the North bank of the Medway estuary.

105. MV HOOCREEK (2)

By the time of this 2003 photograph, the firm had become the major player in UK dry cargo coastal shipping. Specialising in classes of ship, economic to operate and yet capable of taking good sized cargoes into the remaining small ports still open to receive them. This ship belongs to the smaller class and she is one of the Yorkshire Drydock Company's standard design types of the 1980s. The second *Hoocreek* 498g/1,236dwt/1982 is seen here entering Rye Harbour in East Sussex, just a few miles outside the Kent border.

106. North Foreland Lighthouse →

Seen here in the early 1900s, the structure on the North East tip of Thanet remains little altered today. Some form of warning light for shipping has existed here since 1505, when a wooden platform would have supported a 'fire' light, later burning coal. The brick tower dates from 1793 when oil lamps, lenses and reflectors were introduced. 1933 saw the advent of a 3000 watt electric lamp giving a powerful twenty mile range light, one hundred and ninety feet above sea level. Today, in common with modern practice it is unmanned, automated and remotely controlled.

107. Broadstairs in 1906 →

Fish had been landed at Broadstairs in Henry VIII's time and basic wooden piers came and went in the 1700s, smashed by storms. In 1808, the construction of a more substantial pier brought dividends - it lasted. Before the railway's arrival in 1863, coal and building materials were brought ashore on the beach. The Culmer family were leading lights locally and involved in ship building; and in the 1790s, Thomas White was launching hoys such as the *Princess of Wales*, 75 tons. In 1802, with a view to securing Naval contracts to build larger ships, he 'emigrated' to Cowes, Isle of Wight, founding what would become the long lasting 'Whites of Cowes' dynasty of ship builders. Construction of larger craft would simply not have been possible from an exposed beach launch site. The photograph shows a sailing barge rigged in readiness to discharge over the low water period, with a 'shoot' over the side awaiting the carters. As soon as depth of water permits, horses and carts will make short work of dispatching one hundred tons of coal, ashore.

108.   Broadstairs in 2005

This is the modern reverse view to No.107 and shows where the sailing barge had been sitting about halfway between the solitary post and the pier. Today summer pleasure craft prevail.

Map No.9   Ramsgate to Deal →

(1) Ramsgate Continental Ferry Port

(2) Site of the Hovercraft Terminal

(3) Site of Richborough WWI Train Ferry Dock

(4) Site of Richborough WWI Military Port

(5) Sandwich Bridge and Quay

(6) Deal Pier and Timeball Tower

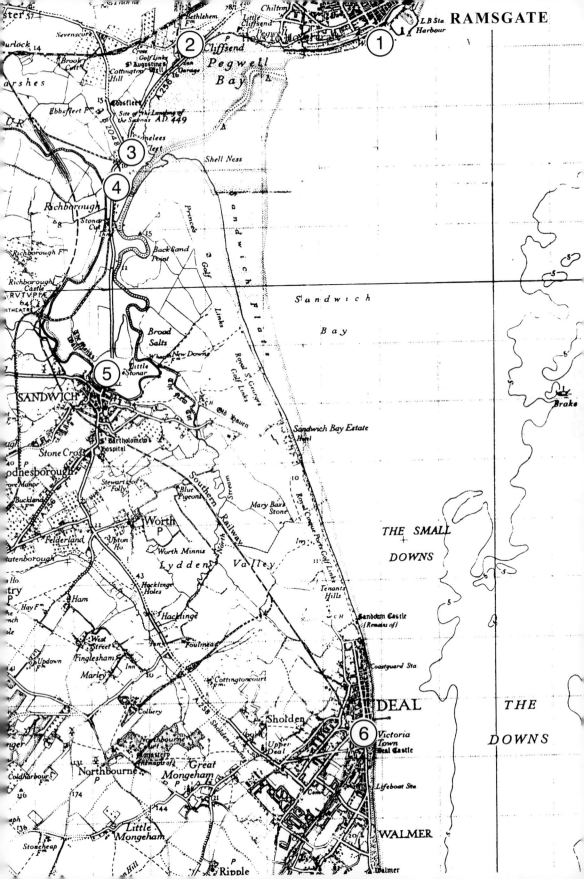

Ramsgate

The Isle of Thanet was indeed just that around 1000 years ago, when the channel of the Wantsume existed from near Reculver on the North Coast, to Sandwich Haven in the east (See Map No. 8.1). Ramsgate developed as a fishing village at a dip in the cliffs where some degree of boat shelter could be found. Nearby, Sandwich had become the 'head port' for the ancient Cinque Ports grouping, yet as trade and shipping expanded, Ramsgate's greater accessibility rendered it of growing importance.

The proximity to the notorious Goodwin Sands would see Ramsgate ever more involved in rescue and salvage work. Stricken craft could be brought into Ramsgate for repair, and this requirement would change but gradually, as steam power and ship reliability improved. The brave local seafarers of Ramsgate, Walmer, Deal and Dover saved thousands of lives between them, from these inhospitable waters.

Ramsgate's harbour construction project was nearing completion in 1773 to local design, when the engineer Smeeton became involved. His expertise had been sought in an endeavour to keep the channels and harbour free of silt, and also to sort out the failed construction of the new drydock. This latter had seemingly been a disaster on commissioning. Between 1786 and the 1791 repairing of the drydock, Smeeton extended the eastern breakwater to help reduce swell in the harbour, which occurred in bad weather.

As early as 1810 some kind of steam dredger helped maintain the harbour depths. In 1824, the General Steam Navigation Company started running steamers from London to Ramsgate, an association with the port that would last for around one hundred and forty years. John Rennie became the next appointed harbour engineer. In 1843 the light tower which still stands on the western breakwater was completed by Shaw.

Coal and timber were the main cargoes handled, and by the mid 1800s a fleet of registered fishing smacks were owned locally. In 1846 Belgian mail (packet) steamers were calling in at the port and in 1865 the permanent lifeboat station opened. Ramsgate also became a regular stop-over point for Brixham trawlers on their way to and from the North Sea fishing grounds. Later, steam trawlers would begin to replace the sailing variety. In 1878, the Sailors Home opened by the harbour to be joined in 1881 by the Smack Boys Home.

This latter institution arose out of the poor conditions prevailing for young trainee deck hands in the fishing industry, locally. Aged from fourteen to twenty, the lads were indentured for five years to the smack owners, to learn their arduous trade. 1889 saw the stationing of the steam paddle tug *Aid* by the Board of Trade. She would be involved in innumerable rescue and salvage operations over the years to come, yet in kinder weather would tow smacks and tripper boats to sea. The drydock, by now long out of use was infilled in 1893.

During WWI the Smack Boys Home closed as smack numbers dwindled, and it never reopened. Ramsgate saw the landing of 43,000 troops from Dunkirk in 1940. After WWII, some coastal trade continued in barges and small motor coasters, often Dutch flagged. In the 1950s Volkswagen chose Ramsgate for their UK importation of cars and in 1973 a new 'finger' jetty opened in the outer harbour for such traffic, which had become 'roll-off' in nature. 1966 saw the start of Hoverlloyd's cross-Channel service with two Westland SRN6 36-seater type hovercraft. By 1969 the operation had expanded to the 250 seater, SRN4 type craft and the facilities for these larger hovercraft were established a mile or two to the west at Pegwell Bay.

1973-75   Thanet Line were running a Ramsgate to Flushing service

1977   Holyman Sally Line were the operators at Ramsgate.

1980   For a few months Ramsgate- Dunkirk Ferries ran the *Nuits St Georges*.
The new, outer ferryport opened to permit the use of larger vessels.

1981   Sally Viking Line were now operating the Dunkirk route.

1983   Pegwell Bay, Ramsgate's International Hovercraft Terminal closes, and all
remaining hovercraft services consolidate at Dover.

1984   The French Schiaffino Line operated a freight only service to Dunkirk.

1996   Sally Line closed their Dartford Terminal, to concentrate at Ramsgate.

1997   Holyman Sally take over the Belgian R.M.T. Ostend services, and *Holyman
Express*, an Incat type fast ferry, is based at Ramsgate.

1999   Holyman departs the scene and Trans Europa Shipping Lines arrive.

2002   Renamed Trans Europa Ferries.

As can be seen here and at other established ferry ports in the South East, there continues to be much change in the industry over the last decade or so. Ramsgate does at least still have its ferry services, some ports do not.

109. The Inner Harbour, 1909

A number of sailing trawlers are moored about the basin, whilst a brigantine appears 'sandwiched' between two barquentines along the Military Road wall. Two items are noticeable by their absence - motor vehicles and private yachts.

110. PT AID

The Board of Trade rescue paddle tug *Aid* 194g/1889 was about as distinctive a craft as could possibly be, with her double ended design layout. She carried steaming lights for each direction and was commanded from the central open bridge. In this 1900s scene she is involved in the fair weather activity of towing a tripper boat out to sea, no doubt a minor income, but some relief from the foul weather rescue and salvage business.

111. NEW MOSS ROSE →

Possibly the subject of Aid's attention in No.110, this beautiful craft is the tripper boat *New Moss Rose* 42r/1899, a gaff rigged cutter seen here in 1912 with a fine load of trippers onboard, one of whom appears to be holding a parasol or umbrella - an item of apparel not generally associated with sailing boats! At this time a day sail to Deal cost one shilling return, time taken – variable, as totally dependent on wind and tide. This vessel had a running mate, a similar craft called *Moss Rose*.

112. Ramsgate Pier Head and a Sailing Trawler →

Shaw's 1843 light tower stands firm on the western breakwater end, although it had been moved back a little, since at first it attracted blows from square rigged ships yardarms, as they entered harbour. In this 1930s view, Ramsgate registered trawler R223 glides out on a north-easterly breeze, off to the fishing grounds. Just discernible to the right of the light tower in the distance is the Sailors Home, and nearby the building that once housed the Smack Boys Home.

113. Pavillion, Pier and Harbour

A typical 1930s holiday scene here has one of the New Medway Steam Packet Company's paddlers tied up to the eastern breakwater. PS *Queen of Kent*, and PS *Queen of Thanet* both 800g/1916, had started life as WWI Naval minesweepers. They could always be recognised by the wide separation of the two funnels. Both went west to the Solent after WWII, to end their careers running for Red Funnel Steamers. Up on the harbour slipway can be seen the stern of a trawler, and the inevitable Watkins tug.

114. ST LOYAL STAR and ST BADIA →

As the old sailing trawlers were withdrawn, a number of steamers took their place in the local fishing fleet. Here, R246 *Loyal Star* 95g/1913 and built at Great Yarmouth, was owned by the Ramsgate Steam Trawling Company. She is tied up to one of Watkin's steam tugs, the *Badia* 150g/1909. This old firm ran a large fleet of ship towage tugs in London, and had used Ramsgate as a base for their Channel and longer distance work for many years. *Badia* was Dartmouth built and one of a class of similar tugs.

115. Steam tugs and a motor coaster →

Beyond the harbour entrance the paddler *Royal Eagle* 1,539g/1932 is underway. On the inner basin cross-wall, a Watkins tug is stoking up, and would appear on the face of things to have suffered some kind of lifeboat davit malfunction – judging by the precarious angle of the hanging boat. To the right is one of the Metcalf Motor Coaster Company's fleet, working cargo. In the 1930s this firm acquired a number of motor ships in the 300 to 500 ton range, precisely described by the Company title. Nearest are a couple more tugs seemingly out of action, and yes, a spritsail barge is awaiting the opening of the dock gate.

116. The Inner Harbour and THE BOUNTY

With WWII not long over, the basin is now devoid of trawlers, and private yachts have yet to proliferate in any numbers. Two very different craft are however, noteworthy. The tiny London River steam pilot tender *Pilot* 39g/1905 is moored under the crane with a canvas cover on her funnel top. Across the harbour over by the famous 1819 Clock House building is the iron hulled barque ex *Alastor* 823g/1875. Built at Sunderland she once traded to New Zealand for Shoreham owners Penneys. Later she went under the Finnish flag and visited the UK in the seasonal Baltic timber trades, in the 1930s. At the outbreak of WWII in 1939 the old ship was trapped in British waters for the duration and used in a static role by the Royal Navy. In 1946 she underwent the 'indignity' of being tarted up as a holiday makers' attraction called *The Bounty*, and duly opened in 1946 at Ramsgate. In 1952, the scrapman dismantled her at Grays, Essex. Iron hulled ships were renowned for great longevity as corrosion works at a fraction of the rate it achieves on steel. Public transport in this 1948 view consists of one double decker bus, and three tourist charabancs of pre-war design. Three or four private cars visible, also pre-war, are black. How things would change, and quickly!

117. MV RAMSGATE →

Captured here in 1963 is the Borough of Ramsgate's motor grab dredger *Ramsgate* 168g/1962. Her job is mundane but essential - keeping the harbour free of silt and transporting the offending substance well offshore to the dumping grounds.

118. MV AUTOSTRADA →

Volkswagens choice of Ramsgate to land their car imports led to the 1973 construction of this concrete apron finger pier into the outer harbour from the cross wall. Specialist vehicle carrying ferries evolved from around 1970 to transport motor cars internationally. The *Autostrada* 610g/1971 was British operated by Uglands of London, and had the capacity for 450 small cars. This advance from lifting cars on and off by traditional crane method, was considerable at the time, and ship turn around time would be drastically reduced. The gross tonnage of this ship is misleading, since it gives no real indication of her overall size, as measured under older tonnage regulations. After twenty five years service *Autostrada* went for scrap in 1996.

119. The New Ferryport

The 1983 built new Continental Ferryport is seen here in full swing. A Sally Line 'Viking' ferry has just departed for Ostend. These ships were of around 4,300 gross tons. The bow of a freight ferry can be seen far left, and the French Schiaffino Lines cargo ferry, *Catherine Schiaffino* 1,583g/1978 lies at a nearby berth. This splendid aerial photograph clearly shows the pier where *Autostrada* had been berthed in the old Outer Harbour.

120. MV GARDENIA →

Sailing out past the Ferryport's rock armour breakwaters in 2005 is Trans Europa Ferries *Gardenia* 8,097g/1978 and once a member of Townsend Thoresen's Dover fleet.

121. MV PRIMROSE →

This 12,110g/1975 built vessel once sailed under the Belgian flag as *Princesse Marie Christine*. Here she is about to turn around on arrival at Ramsgate before moving astern to the linkspan, beyond which the cooling towers of the redundant Richborough power station can be seen, a few miles away. *Primrose* was rebuilt in 1998 with extra stability enhancing 'waterline side tanks' as required by International Rule changes.

122. MT BALTIC STEVNS

Seen here in 2005 moored against Ramsgate's eastern breakwater is the distinctive form of an ex German, Bugsier Company tug. Originally in black and white livery in her Hamburg days she now has a green hull with yellow upperworks. *Bugsier 26*, had been the earlier name. As previously noted, tugs have been a feature of the Ramsgate area more or less ever since their invention. The busy nearby shipping lanes can still on occasion throw up maritime mishaps at short notice - requiring a tug's immediate attention.

123. ST CERVIA and the Drydock →

The preserved Watkins steam tug *Cervia* 233g/1946 overlooks the partially reclaimed and restored drydock. Out of use by the 1880s, Smeetons drydock had been made into an ice store for the local fishing industry, but in 1923 this function was no longer required and the dock covered over. Today, the ex Danish wooden fishing vessel *Lola of Strandby* sits in the dock. She last fished out of Hartlepool as *HL7 Strandby* and had been built at Esbjerg in 1941, measuring in at 25 gross tons. A large navigation buoy perched on the dock wall completes the 2005 scene.

124. MV RAMSGATE in 2005 →

Working in between the yacht mooring pontoons is the subject of No.117, still employed on the same essential maintenance tasks as over forty years earlier. Quite remarkable, in fast changing times.

125. GRAND TURK in the Marina

Moored just where many a square rigger has in days gone by, the replica frigate *Grand Turk* 314g/1996 looks the part. Later in the year (2005), she would be centre stage in the Nelson 200 celebrations off Southsea. Note how in the intervening years the ever growing popularity of small boats has just about filled the basin. Far right can be seen the Clock House building which houses Ramsgate's splendid Maritime Museum. The drydock and ST *Cervia* are just in front thereof. See No.116 for comparison view.

126. 'Old boats' →

Further along the quay from the Grand Turk are three very different traditional wooden hulled boats. The nearest craft 78CK is the smack *Mary of Colchester*, dating from 1844 and reportedly rebuilt twice since. The white hulled yacht is the *Emanuel* of 1928, and the larger black hulled vessel is the wooden motor fishing vessel (MFV) *Morayshire*, of Inverness.

Pegwell Bay

Few places hold such historical interest. The Romans landed nearby in A.D.43. Hengist and his warriors landed at Ebbsfleet in AD449, and in AD 597 Augustine and his Monks similarly passed this way. The broad shallow area offshore was long known as Sandwich Haven, but given centuries of sea level changes, coastal erosion and siltation, the haven's profile drastically altered. Today the area is better known as Pegwell Bay from the mouth of the River Stour, seawards. At one time a small pier existed at Pegwell for local pleasure craft and the nearby International Hovercraft Terminal came and went in something less than two decades.

127. Ramsgate International Hoverport

Not long after its short move westwards from Ramsgate Harbour, Hoverlloyd's smart new purpose built terminal is seen here up and running in the early 1970s. On the tarmac is *Sir Christopher* one of the SRN4 hovercraft, dating from 1972. Initially these craft could carry 250 passengers and 35 cars, but following a 'stretching' operation in 1978/9 this would rise to 390 passengers and 55 cars. The boarding caravan appears in grave danger of grazing its rear parts on the ground. Sadly, this state of the art facility would be short lived indeed, as all hovercraft services went to Dover in the 1980s.

Richborough WWI Port

Ship size seldom exceeded 300 tons apiece before 1800 in both Naval and Merchant operation. Sandwich Haven had coped up to that time but in the 19th century ship sizes increased as indeed their tonnages still continue to escalate today. By the mid 1800s, the Royal Navy had its sights fixed on a deepwater harbour to be purpose built down the coast at Dover. This would be free of winding channels and their propensity for rapid siltation.

Around 1910 a flurry of interest arose at Richborough when coal seams were locally discovered, however these proved shallow in nature and uneconomic to extract. Other more significant coal finds in Kent would later lead to the ever optimistic East Kent Light Railway pushing a new line from its small empire over the main line to Richborough, to ship coal from Shepherdswell Colliery.

In 1914, the Government War Department needed a suitably large site to marshal and shift vast quantities of war material cross-Channel to France. Richborough, through new rail connections to the main line and many new sidings, could handle such traffic. Barge building yards were constructed either side of a loop in the River Stour towards Sandwich. Some 183 barges would duly be launched at these makeshift slipways, of a size suited for use through the French canals and their locks.

Almost 2,000,000 tons of war effort material travelled this way cross-Channel and onwards. Some 400,000 tons of salvaged equipment would duly return after the 1918 armistice. This was some achievement for tug towed barges of a maximum 267 ton capacity each. Reportedly not a single tug or barge was lost at sea.

To support the barge loading operation, a brand new steel piled wharf, 2374ft in length was hurriedly built at Richborough. State of the art rail mounted electric gantry cranes could 'plumb' rail wagons and barge holds. To greatly accelerate the movement of rail mounted items in 1916, the Government ordered what would become the first proper purpose built, seagoing train ferry steamers. A special linkspan berth was dredged out and the river channel straightened and provided with a 'turning circle' for the ships. The shore end of the berth was served by many railway sidings.

It appears that once the last homeward shipment of salvaged gear arrived in 1919, the entire site went into decline. The much anticipated coal export bonanza did not live up to expectations, although some Military activity would return during WWII. This involved the preparation of floating roadways for the Mulberry Harbour project, so Richborough saw further use of its workshops, and some landing craft activity.

Briefly, in the early 1930s the Southern Railway looked at the site potential to establish their cross-Channel train ferry operation. Richborough lost out in preference to deep water Dover, with its fast established rail links - a sensible choice given the Stour's shifting, silty nature. In 1936 the Dover-Dunkirk train ferry service began running, but more of that later.

Richborough Train Ferries

The berth for the ships was not ready until February 1918, almost the end of the War. The three ships had been built between 1916/17, two coming from Armstrong Whitworth's, Newcastle yard, and one from Fairfield Shipbuilding, Glasgow. They were given the suitably austere names of TF 1, TF 2 & TF 3. Substantially constructed steamers they measured 364ft loa by 59ft br by 10ft dr. and were quite clearly of a 'ground breaking' design for their time. Side by side twin boiler uptakes and funnels enabled the twin rail connection over the stern to branch out into four siding lines onboard. Boilers were oil fired and twin screws powered by triple expansion engines gave a service speed of 12 knots. Gross tonnages were around 2,600 each. Passengers were not carried and the ships also shared another route - Southampton-Dieppe. A fourth train ferry ran briefly between Southampton and Cherbourg, but this was a conversion from a merchant ship.

The Richborough ferries served until the end of 1919, at which point the South Eastern and Chatham Railway showed a brief interest in the port, but took no further action. After this time there appears to have been some wrangling over the site, but terminal decline had set in by 1923, when Railway 'Grouping' occurred. However, perhaps some far sighted individual had spotted how successful the train ferries were at carrying motor vehicles, and had a glimpse of the future? It would be some decades later that public car ownership and aspiration to drive on the continent, would manifest itself.

Duly, the London and North Eastern Railway Company purchased the three ferries, a gantry and a linkspan, for what would become their long lived Harwich to Zeebrugge train ferry service. The ships were 'slightly' renamed - *Train Ferry No.1* etc. Most surprisingly, the LNER then converted the ships to coal firing. In WWII they were again pressed into Naval service which, sadly saw *Train Ferry Nos 2 & 3* lost. The old *TF 1*, survived under British Railways control as *Essex Ferry* not going for scrap until 1957, when a new ship of the same name entered service

128. A 'TF' to unload

One of the three ferries is seen here gently nudging astern into the rail linkspan berth at Richborough. On this trip army road vehicles salvaged for home disposal seem to outnumber rail trucks. The two rail connections branching out to the four lines on deck are under the first vehicle, and mens' feet. This specialist berth and facility had a working life of less than two years.

129. The New Wharf, Richborough →

The 2374ft long straight quay is in full swing here, with numerous barges alongside and rail trucks waiting unloading. The whole ensemble could easily pass as a modern rail connected container port facility. Evidently dredging of the Stour had not quite been completed, and even here a distant sprit sail barge is doing its bit for the War effort.

130. The ex Train Ferry Dock in 2005 →

Some eighty six years after its brief wartime heyday, a line of rusting steel piles and some decaying wooden stumps are all that remain, as nature re-asserts ownership of the site. The River Stour still wanders past, always seeking the short way out to sea, with its changing channels and mudbanks. The old railway company's decision to use Dover for their train ferry operation need no longer be questioned.

131.   TRAIN FERRY No3, at Harwich

Peace time in the 1930s and the old *TF3* is in commercial service between Harwich and Zeebrugge . The four lines of rail wagons can clearly be seen in this departing view. Nevertheless, the ship is fundamentally unaltered from WWI days. The last of the trio to survive, *TF1*, did receive some modifications in later days as *Essex Ferry* and went for scrap in 1957 with one central funnel, in lieu of the athwartship pair of twin stacks.

132.   Site of the Military Port, 2005

The long line of trees mark the inner edge of the WWI New Wharf, and long gone are the gantry cranes, railway sidings and barge activity. The grassy area here infilled with boat boardwalks, was once part of the waterway adjacent to the train ferry berth - behind the camera.

133. Stonar Cut

Here today, a solitary house-boat barge sits on its own mudbank. The cut beneath links two loops of the River Stour, and was put in to aid drainage in the 1700s. To the left, (seaward) of the barge, stood the workshops and administration block for the New Wharf WWI project.

Sandwich and The Cinque Ports

The original Cinque Ports were Hastings, Sandwich, Dover, Hythe and Romney, and for a thousand years they were truly in the front line for any prospective invader. In pre Navy days, each coastal town was charged with providing ships to the King for defence of the realm. Later, other 'limb' ports joined in the arrangements. From William the Conqueror's time a Lord Warden of the Cinque Ports held office. In 1229 Henry III stipulated that fifty seven ships should serve for fifteen days per year.

The towns so involved were given certain privileges for their trouble - some degree of self governance. By the time of the Spanish Armada the Cinque Port confederation was already in decline, since a permanent and expanding Royal Navy had been formed. Today, the role of Lord Warden remains, being largely ceremonial and allied to the historic nature of the old Cinque Ports tradition. Several of the original Cinque Ports have long since become land-locked by coastal deposition and shingle drift. eg Romney and Winchelsea.

Sandwich, as we have already seen, could at certain periods in its history, accept ships up to about 300 tons. In the 1850s, small brigs and schooners were trading to its quays, but by the middle of the 20th century, sailing barges and motor coasters of around 200 tons could berth. However, as the ship sizes increased, visits grew less frequent to the port, and the point was reached several decades ago when commercial ships could no longer visit the Town quays. Yachting and boating pursuits continue for as long as the Stour permits sufficient depth of water in its channels.

In the late 1800s sailing barges were built here in some numbers, and the following were still trading in 1934. Henry Felton constructed many: *Agnes Mary* 50r/1894, *Alaric* 73r/1901, *Colonia* 62r/1897, *Gladys* 64r/1900, *John Bayly* 56r/1895, *Maggie* 63r/1898, *Mayor* 70r/1899, *Lord Warden* 50r/1891, *Snowdrop* 55r/1893, *Tollesbury* 70r/1901, *Trilby* 53r/1896, and *Winifred* 66r/1893.

Sandwich's splendid old swing bridge dates similarly (1891), and perhaps unsurprisingly finally required a new operating mechanism in 1993. Cargoes once handled hereabouts were coal, (domestic and gasworks), timber, beer and agricultural produce.

← 134. Sandwich by air

This fine aerial view, probably from the 1920s, highlights a complete lack of vegetation on the opposite bank to the town. No less than four ships may be observed working cargo at the various wharves above and below the swing bridge. The sailing barge in the foreground is most likely unloading gasworks coal as she is close to that facility. The retort house and gasometer are clearly visible. The narrow river width and lack of depth have always dictated the dimensions of locally built, and visiting ships over the centuries.

135. ST SANDWICH and DORCAS

A busy scene of commerce around 1910, and the Borough of Sandwich's little steam tug *Sandwich* 26g/1892 is hard at work. She was built at Millwall and registered at Ramsgate when locally employed. Under tow is the East Kent Brewery Company's barge *Dorcas* 72r/1898 and she has evidently been to their upstream wharf. This old barge with its distinctive broad white hull band, would be rebuilt at Greenwich in 1921 trading on under the delightful name of *Squeak*. The tug has some extras onboard enjoying a trip down to the sea, and at least the skipper will avoid sunburn or a shower by the stretched canvas cover overhead. Whilst *Sandwich* has steam to spare for the run downriver, some pedestrians will be hoping for a quick closure of the bridge.

136. HENDERIKA by the Gasworks

The steel hulled Dutch schooner appears all but frozen in by the quayside in this undated wintry scene. Craft of this type were rare after WWII, so it may have been much earlier than the deep freeze of Winter 1947. *Henderika* 198g/1917 is typical of many Dutch auxiliary powered vessels, and for many decades these little ships were almost as common in minor United Kingdom ports as they were at home. The gasworks retort house and gasometer seen in the earlier aerial view, are silhouetted in this down river view from the bridge.

137. MV ESPERANCE at Sandwich ↗

Busily unloading timber from the Baltic in this mid 1950s scene is the tiny Dutch motor coaster *Esperance* 163g/1930, and already trading on her third name. These handy little ships traded around most of North West Europe's coasts and were often owned and run by the captain and his family members, living permanently onboard. The custom would die out in the 1960s as commercial pressures and industrial changes brought this fascinating way of life to a close. The wheeled device pressed into service for shifting timber is believed to be an ex wartime bomb trolley - nothing wasted here.

138. Sandwich Quay in 2005 →

Leisure craft and homes replace earlier industry, but the Bell Hotel still presides. The once barren land opposite now supports verdant undergrowth and mature tree specimens.

139.   Deal Beach in 1840 →

This delightful pen and inkwash scene comes from the sketchbook of Henry Moses (c1782-1870) and clearly illustrates Deal's close involvement with shipping in the Downs and nearby Goodwins. Whilst a three masted barque sails by, other ships lie beyond, and one of the local luggers is just offshore. A Deal galley rests on the beach stern on to the sea, next to a more substantial lugger. These craft between them, and many similar around the English coasts, were the rescue boats of their day, before the inception of the permanent lifeboat service.

140.   PRIDE OF THE SEA ↘

Here lies the sad remains of the lugger *Pride of the Sea* wrecked in a gale off the Isle of Wight in 1887. She has come ashore with the bottom frames clearly visible through a large hole in her side. The folk visible are locals, no doubt with thoughts of firewood. They came from the same background hereabouts, and also understood the power of the sea, and its effects. See Deal notes concerning this lugger.

Deal, The Downs and The Goodwins

Between Deal and the treacherous Goodwin Sands lies a 'safer' deep area known as The Downs. This channel is sheltered by land from the prevailing westerlies, and to some extent from easterlies, by the Goodwins. Vast fleets of outward bound merchant sailing ships would anchor here to await a northerly, or easterly wind to take them down Channel, and beyond. Many passing ships and some dragging their anchor, were claimed by the Goodwins, whose shifting sands quickly removed all traces of wreckage in short order. Deal's seafarers, traditionally fishermen, were often called upon to launch their boats in foul weather to assist or rescue ships' crews. Their reputation for bravery and fine seamanship became legendary, as they put to sea in their luggers and galleys.

Another service rendered involved taking several pilots at a time, down Channel, to place them on incoming merchantmen. Again a most hazardous occupation and not, over the decades, without some considerable loss of life to the boatmen. The Deal luggers were the further ranging craft, stoutly constructed and over 30ft loa, they were in the 20-25 ton range - quite large for beach launched vessels. The design provided for a very seaworthy craft indeed, and when fully rigged they originally had three masts and lugsails. The centre mast appears to have fallen out of favour as it hampered deck working space, so tended to be left out, latterly, particularly when fishing.

Galleys were smaller, lighter construction , five oared pulling craft, but could still set one central mast and a lugsail. This type was long, narrow and shallow, and it is said could be easily dragged over the Goodwins, if needs must. Some examples of this type of beach built and launched boat lasted until WWI. The following are examples of tragic loss due to storms far from home in the English Channel. The brave souls involved would probably have been trying to put pilots on ships inbound. Tired Captains and Crews relied upon the pilot's expert local knowledge through the narrow confines of the Dover Strait.

Pride of the Sea	lost at Luccombe, Isle of Wight	1882
Walmer Castle	lost at Ventnor, Isle of Wight	1892
Petrel *	lost off Start Point, Devon	1887

* This lugger was duly recovered, salvaged and returned, only to lose another crew five years later, when renamed *Walmer Castle*.

141. A Sailing Lifeboat in 1906

Following the establishment of the Royal National Lifeboat Service in the 1860s, the first craft were sailing and pulling types. Here we see Deal's double ended, self-righting, pulling boat setting off under sail in a brisk breeze towards the Goodwins. The crew are well prepared in sou'westers, oil skins and the cork lifejackets of the day. On occasion a steam tug would tow a lifeboat out to the scene of a rescue, but shortly lifeboats would become motorised. Some steam lifeboats were built in the 1890s, but this could hardly have been the best propulsion system, given the time necessary to raise steam.

142. The Timeball tower →

Once time pieces had evolved to the accuracy required for onboard calculation of longitude, it became necessary to correct chronometers to Greenwich Mean Time (GMT). A few seconds error onboard a ship making landfall after an ocean passage could have very serious implications, indeed. In 1833 at Greenwich a 'time-ball' similar to the one on the right, was 'dropped' down its pole at precisely 1300 Local Time, each day. Ships masters, within sight thereof on the Thames, could set their chronometers for the voyage ahead. The Deal timeball, highly visible to mariners out in The Downs, was duly connected by wire to Greenwich Observatory in 1854, quite an advanced notion in pre radio days. The Signal Tower pre dates this to 1821, and now houses the Timeball Museum, open in summer.

143. Deal Pier

Replacing an earlier structure, this modern minimalist pier duly opened in 1957, one of the last built. Today it is much used by fishermen, the original idea behind seaside piers has faded into memory, as they were principally steamer boarding jetties, and for the Victorians to partake in 'promenading'. Most of the remaining traditional piers could now no longer receive ships, as the end staging necessary to berth them, has long gone. Additionally, the excursion ships have largely departed, save for a couple in preservation and some small local craft in popular areas.

Map No.10   South Foreland to Dover Harbour

(1)   South Foreland Lighthouse
(2)   Aerial ropeway from Tilmanstone Colliery
(3)   Dover Eastern Docks
(4)   Prince of Wales Pier and the 'Hover' Terminal
(5)   Inner Basins
(6)   Admiralty Pier - modern Cruise Ship Terminals.

144. South Foreland Lighthouse

Fires were reportedly lit in cliff caves to warn shipping as early as 1367. The present tower stands three hundred and seventy four feet above sea level, dates from 1843 and has a light range of some twenty five miles out over the Dover Strait.

145. MV FERROCRETE →

This smart little motor ship 158g/1927 came from J. Pollock's Faversham Shipyard. For many years she ran in the service of the Associated Portland Cement Company. A regular voyage in her cement carrying days was as running mate to the barge *Celtic* on the Sussex to Isle of Wight bagged cement trade. In the 1950s photograph she appears immaculate, as if from annual overhaul.

146. MV LEASPRAY →

The original name of this sturdy little motor ship was *Goldace* 199g/1932 and she was yet another product of Faversham Shipyard. By the time of this 1950s view taken beneath the white cliffs, Sullys of Bridgwater, Somerset, were operating her.

← 147. ALAN

Built at Battersea in 1900, the 61reg.ton *Alan* last worked for the London and Rochester Company. She is specially included here to illustrate the true meaning of auxiliary power. The conversion to motor propulsion has seen the installation of a small wheelhouse, loss of the mizzen mast and removal of the bowsprit. In the 1950s photograph the topmast is lowered and she can still set a fore, and mainsail. The Thames side scene has her carrying a deck load of sawn timber, a common job and probably from the Surrey Commercial Docks round to the Medway. She still needs her leeboards, and would manage to see in the new century, as a house boat.

↙ 148. MB CONVOY

Built at Rye, East Sussex the Dover registered *Convoy* 73r/1900 started out as a typical wooden hulled coastal sailing barge. The image, in a similar location to the previous, shows the transition to full motor ship status. A rather more substantial wheelhouse and cabin have been built aft to replace the space below, lost to the engine department. In *Convoy's* case the transition occurred in 1944 and no vestige of sailing apparel remains.

Dover Historical

Such have been the changes witnessed at this famous location that a summary timescale of events may be helpful. Dover's closeness to Continental Europe has placed it in the forefront of travel and trade, for over two thousand years. In Roman times, the mouth of the little River Dour was believed to offer some form of sheltered harbour, and a landing place gap in the cliffs. As early as 1495 it seems that coastal changes rendered the anchorage unsatisfactory, and the first attempt a little to the westward, was made to construct an 'artificial' harbour. Within a century or two, these docks were reportedly blocked. In 1606, the Lord Warden of the Cinque Ports had responsibility for the harbour. It is believed that before 1686 small, fast gaff cutters were plying the routes to Ostend and Calais with mails - the first 'packet' boats.

By 1750, three working dock basins had been built. Between 1793 and 1815 communications to France largely ceased, owing to the French internal matter of 'The Revolution'. Normal mail services were quickly restored after the Battle of Waterloo. 1820 saw the paddle steamer *Rob Roy* 90 tons, and of 30HP start running a service from Dover. She was built by Denny of Dumbarton. In 1822 J. Hayward of Dover had two 100 ton, 40HP steamers operating and, by 1836 no less than five ships were carrying Post Office mails, on the Ostend run. The Railway reached Dover Town in 1843 but not until 1862 would the Lords of the Admiralty permit trains to enter the Port area. Between 1847 and 1897 various improvements were made to basins and piers, whilst an Act of Parliament first conceived the Dover Harbour Board in 1861.

1874 saw entry into service of the PS *Castalia* – the first twin hulled, four funnelled steamer. Of 290ft loa by 60ft br. she could manage 11kts, but was not deemed much of a success. The next year saw the Admiralty Pier brought into service. In 1878 a more advanced steamer, similar to the *Castalia*, began running as *Calais-Douvres No.1*. In 1881, Parliamentary consent was given for the 'first' Channel tunnel, leading to coal being found at the Shakespeare Cliff workings. This gave rise to the short lived Dover Colliery which suffered from poor coal output. 1882 saw a return to a more traditional design of cross Channel ferry in the form of PS *Invicta*, 1,197grt capable of 18kts. The period 1895-98 saw the last ever batch of paddle steamers for the route enter service - *Duchess of York* 996grt, *Princess of Wales* 1,009grt, *Mabel Grace* 1,215 grt and *Lord Warden*.

The turbine steamship era arrived in 1902 with the introduction of SS *Queen* and ship sizes were increasing as evidenced by this ship's dimensions of 323ft loa by 43ft.br. In 1904 Trans-Atlantic liners began calling at Dover en route Europe-USA. By 1907 the turbine powered ferries prevailed with *Onward*, *Victoria*, *Empress* & *Invicta* all in service. 1909 King George V opened the Admiralty Harbour. A 'broadened' Admiralty Pier, created by reclaiming land from the harbour, opened for public use as Dover Marine Station in 1919, although the site had been used for hospital trains during WWI. In 1923 the Dover Harbour Board took over port control.

The Townsend family, who had been involved in ocean shipping since the 1880s, took the first tentative step towards specialist cross-Channel vehicle transportation. A typical small steam coaster the *Artificer* was chartered in 1928, and 15 cars could be craned on and off. Any passengers more than the BOT regulatory 12 had to travel by separate steam ferry, to be reunited with their cars on the other side. In 1929 rather unsurprisingly, the Southern Railway observed this development, and started their service in similar style.

1930 found the port reached by an aerial ropeway seven miles from the Tilmanstone Colliery. At a rate of 120 tons per hour, its coal bucket delivery system would stock a purpose built bunker holding 5,000 tons on the Eastern breakwater. Ships could load by telescopic shoot at rates between 500-750 tph. This whole ensemble became redundant by WWII, and awaited dismantling in 1954. Southern Railway, too, had their own coal bunkers and the Shell Oil Company had some 10,000 tons storage capacity at the old Admiralty eastern site. In the 1930s apart from the cross-Channel traffic, Dover handled coal, grain, timber and general cargo.

Townsend converted the WWI type minesweeper HMS *Forde* 829g/1919 in 1930 for the carriage of 200 passengers and 34 cars - the race was on! The following year Southern Railway brought in their 'adapted' cargo ship *Autocarrier* 822g/1931, she had been fitted with an additional lounge and refreshment area, however cars were still craned onboard. Excess passengers still went by traditional ferry.

1936 saw the long awaited introduction of the Dover to Dunkirk train ferry service. SS *Shepperton Ferry*, *Twickenham Ferry* & *Hampton Ferry*, all 2,839grt and 360ft loa by 61ft.br they would use the 'tailor-made' train ferry dock for the next three decades, or so. This route would become famous for the Night Ferry service. In reality the ships were updated versions of the Richborough WWI 'TF's in design. Twelve railway coaches or forty wagons could be carried, and an 'upper' garage deck could also take 30 cars.

More generally at Dover in the 1930s Cross Channel services were-

Passenger	Dover to Calais	twice	daily
	Dover to Ostend	thrice	daily
Cargo	To both ports		daily

P. Hawksfield of Dover ran several steam coasters and Dover Navigation of London registered their cargo steamers at Dover.

After WWII and some recuperation, both Townsend and the Southern Railway grasped the nettle with regard to the public's increasing desire to go motoring on the Continent. Townsend acquired the redundant WWII frigate SS *Halladale* 1,370g/1944 and of 301ft loa and 36ft br. Twin steam turbine powered she was given a proper stern gate access to the car deck. 368 passengers and 55 cars could then travel together at 20 kts. The drive-on era had begun, but as yet at only one end of the ship. British Railways duly responded with full conversion of their popular twin funnelled steam ferry *Dinard* giving a 368 passenger, 70 car limit. By the 1960s the days of traditional steamers were nearing their end, and a number were variously converted to car ferry mode, thereby extending their working lives. However, the motor ships were in the ascendancy.

1967 saw Townsend bring in another converted ship, this time the ex General Steam Navigation's excursion ferry *Royal Sovereign* 1,851g/1948, a twin screw 20 kt motor ship. She entered the car ferry business under the old railway name of *Autocarrier*, thence sailing on the Zeebrugge route until 1973. British Railways took a mighty leap into the unknown in 1969 with a Hovercraft service to Calais from a new purpose built Hoverport, using SRN4 craft capable of 50 kts. More generally, in the 1970s the few remaining passenger-only ships were phased out, and all operators brought in newer, bigger vessels. In 1976, typically there were some 80 ferry and 13 hovercraft movements per day, at Dover.

That year a new operator appeared on the scene in the form of P&O, who arrived with a single ship, the *Lion* 3,987g/1967 to compete on the Boulogne route. Capable of carrying 1038 passengers and 160 cars she would later be joined by *Tiger* and *Panther*. By 1980 the independent French freight only operator Schiaffino Lines started running to Ostend. The Calais 'hover' crossing was under the Seaspeed banner and the very last steam turbine passenger ferry *Caesarea* (ex- Weymouth) sailed. In 1984 after privatisation, the old British

Rail livery vanished under Sealink's control - a new blue and white colour scheme appeared.

In 1988, work started, this time for real, on the Channel Tunnel construction site and this would herald a rather unsettling period for all the ferry operators, pondering their long term future. Seafrance brought in a brand new combined road and train ferry service to Dunkirk, to be run not from the old train ferry dock, but a special new double linkspan berth along the Admiralty Pier. This vessel was named *Nord Pas De Calais*, the service lasted until the Channel Tunnel operations settled down, when the ship went over to road haulage vehicle work.

After various competition investigations, P&O and Stena Line merged their Dover operations in 1997. A new, second Cruise Ship Terminal opened along the Admiralty Pier in 2001. The hovercraft were totally withdrawn to be replaced by fast 'surface effect' vessels. The existing Hoverport was given a linkspan type berth for this changeover, adjacent to the base of the Prince of Wales Pier. Norfolk Line, a newcomer, began running to Dunkirk. And in 2004 Speedlines started an 'Incat' fast service to Dunkirk. By 2005 further new roll-on, roll-off berths opened, to accept the largest ferries on the various services.

149. A 'Packet' arriving
Taken from an 1819 lithograph, this delightful image shows a gaff cutter entering Dover Harbour between the rudimentary wooden piers. A ketch has just set off to tack its way seaward, and along by the breakwater an inshore fishing lugger is bouncing out to sea. To the right is a signal station and beyond, as ever, the Castle looks on from its lofty perch. In the foreground a couple of fishermen chew the fat, as ever.

150. PS PRINCESS MAUD and ONDINE

This is an unknown artist's impression of a race that took place between these two paddle steamers in 1844. Rivalry is nothing new in the business of courting passengers on the fiercely competitive Channel crossing. Below deck weather protection was the only kind on offer in those pioneering steamship days.

151. PS CALAIS-DOUVRES No.1 →

This radically designed ferry did not prove quite so clever in service. The London, Chatham & Dover Railway Company's 1,820g/1877 built, twin hulled steamer, could muster 600HP. Boilers and engines were in both hulls with the paddle wheels in between the two seventeen foot wide hull sections. The ship could manage 13kts, but reliability and handling were deemed too problematic, and she was withdrawn in 1887 as too slow. *Calais-Douvres* No.2 reverted to traditional paddle steamer design, and could achieve 22kts. The photograph shows old No.1 hidden in a dock corner.

152. Admiralty Pier in the 1900s →

Only paddlers are visible here at berths inside and outside the Admiralty Pier, well before WW1. Just before that War, major infill work was undertaken in the area where the two paddle streamers are moored, giving additional rail lines and ultimately, Dover Marine Station. The three ships visible are representatives of that last ever batch of cross Channel paddle ferries built. Close observation reveals the 'hauling-off' wires by way of which each ship could ease away from the berth on departure.

153. Granville Dock

The Faversham registered barge *Edward* 45r/1881 and Sittingbourne built, lies alongside, and across the water; three railway paddlers are visible in lay-up. Two of these are over the wall in the Wellington Dock. A typical Scandinavian white hulled wooden barque is moored opposite - such craft were the tramp ships of their day. Beyond the barque appears to be a high stack of logwood, possibly pit props. The photograph dates from the 1900s.

154. The Commercial Harbour →

Viewed from the 'Heights' around 1910, this scene takes in Granville Dock and the Tidal Basin plus a good part of the Western Harbour. It is packed full of interesting craft. In the distance dredgers and steam hoppers lie at anchor, whilst in the Tidal Basin near the rectangular shape of the famous Lord Warden Hotel, two railway cargo steamers are moored. Far left a spritsail barge awaits entry to the Wellington Dock. In the Granville Dock two of the turbine ferries are moored together and a Clyde Shipping Company black liveried passenger/cargo ship is raising steam. A topsail schooner and a very early railway cargo steamer, lie in the foreground. In the line-up of craft moored stern on to the dock wall, can be seen one of the Admiralty's steam paddle tugs.

155. SS ALASTAIR and a 'tug-of-war'. →

Another scene from the 1900s, with the Aberdeen steam coaster *Alastair* 366g/1902 sitting peacefully at her berth, whilst nearby there is much straining of backs and oars, watched by a crowd. Two large 'whaler' type boats are engaged in a fierce tug of war with shirt sleeved rowers doing their utmost to win. Perhaps this might have been some kind of annual event? Note the vertically boilered steam crane on the work barge.

156. IRON QUEEN

This time one of the newer turbine powered ferries lies opposite to a brigantine owned by Edward Crundall, of Dover. *Iron Queen* came from a Newport, Monmouthshire shipyard in 1865.

157. ST LADY BRASSEY →

Of 352g/1913 built, this fine old twin funnelled steam tug came from J.P. Rennoldson's, South Shields Shipyard, to the order of Dover Harbour Board. For the following forty five years she would serve them well, performing such duties as passenger ship tender, salvage vessel, towage in the Channel, and the more mundane mud hopper towing to sea. She saw Admiralty service in both World Wars and finally went for scrap in 1958.

158. SS RIVIERA →

In 1911, the South Eastern and Chatham Railway ordered this 1,783grt turbine steamer from Dumbarton. 1923 saw the railway companies 'grouped' and all the local ships came under Southern Railway's control. *Riviera* would give her new operators a further ten years service, before going north-west to join Burns & Laird Lines as *Lairds Isle*.

159. SS ISLE OF THANET

All of the Denny of Dumbarton railway steamers had a kind of 'family of ships' design similarity, evolved over many decades. The *Isle of Thanet* 2,701g/1925 surely had the cleanest lines. Side alleyways are no longer open to the elements and service speeds are now mostly above the 20 knot barrier, enabling tight boat train connections to be made both sides of the Channel. The photograph dates from the 1950s, as radar has been fitted.

160. MS PORT HUON →

With low cloud up around Dover Castle, Port Lines veteran refrigerated cargo motor ship *Port Huon* 8,524g/1927 pauses off the breakwaters with pilot ladder at the ready. For her date of construction this was a large motor ship indeed. Note the safety rope from the forecastle head to the bridge deck, to accompanying the pilot ladder. One of the Trinity House pilot vessels may just be made out in the gloom of the harbour, above the ship's funnel.

161. SS PETER HAWKSFIELD →

P. Hawksfield and Son, of Dover ran several steam coasters in the 1930s. Here the 959g/1918 built steamer has derricks raised ready for cargo work. Even in the late 1930s some steam coasters still had open bridges - although this particular ship does have good sized lookout 'boxes' for shelter. The ship began trading as the *Ralph Harrison* from her Dundee shipyard origins, and would not join the Dover registry until 1929.

162. SS SEA GLORY

The London firm of ship owners, Dover Navigation Ltd chose to register their fleet of tramp steamers in the port of Dover. In a 1930s unknown setting, their *Sea Glory* 1,966g/1919 seems to be in lay-up, as there is a complete lack of smoke, steam, cooling water outlet, or any form of onboard activity visible. Many ships suffered a lack of trade at this time.

163. SS ARTIFICER →

Already briefly mentioned, this unremarkable little steamer 386g/1905, had the 'honour' of becoming, albeit briefly, Townsend's first car ferry. She had been built for well known shipowners, 'T' Coasters Ltd. Her short career on the Dover cross-Channel service would see her taking 15 cars per trip. These were handled on and off by wooden trays supported by slings, during the ship's 1928 sojourn at Dover. A stage hangs below the name on the bow, which has just been repainted.

164. SS AUTOCARRIER →

In this 1930s scene car embarkation and disembarkation was still 'aerial', by dockside crane. This 822g/1931 built ship became Southern Railway's first serious foray into cross-Channel car traffic. Interestingly, by 1928 purpose built double ended car ferries had been introduced by Southern Railway on the Portsmouth to Fishbourne (IOW) route, but these were tiny vessels, in sheltered waters. Although the image is a little unclear, several black cars can be made out on the quayside, awaiting their turn for the crane. Compare this ship to No.190 and the modifications from straight cargo ship design can be seen.

165. SS FORDE

Once the Naval minesweeper HMS *Ford*, at 821g/1919 this ship joined the merchant ranks with Townsend in 1930. She had accommodation for 200 passengers and 34 cars and by the time of this photograph, a basic stern gate had been fitted, rendering car loading by crane a thing of the past. One motor coach has backed up to the boat deck limit for height, and the other will have to reverse off, before much else can happen, on arrival at Calais. Rather surprisingly in the background through the smoke, SS *Invicta* 4,178g /1940 appears about to receive a car into her fore hold, in the old crane manner, whilst raising steam.

166. SS SHEPPERTON FERRY →

Of 2,996grt and 1935 built, this ship was one of the three brought in to run the Dunkirk train ferry service, from 1936. The overall design and layout closely follows the earlier Richborough '*TFs*' of 1916. Two shore rail connections fan out into four onboard rail lines on the train deck. Of course, much more accommodation has been provided, yet the twin uptakes and after docking bridge remain as before. The block beneath the mainmast is the 30 car garage. The photograph shows the ship moving astern to her special 'dock' at Dover in the 1950s, which enabled loading and unloading to progress, without worry about tide height.

167. SS HALLADALE →

Unable to totally shed the earlier 'frigate' image, this ex- Royal Navy ship had been brought in by Townsend in 1950. Of 1,370grt and 1944 built, she is seen here after conversion to car ferry, edging out of the old Eastern Dock. The submarine pens would soon go in deference to increasing demand for vehicle transportation. Also visible here along the arm are the pylons that once held the Tilmanstone Colliery ropeway. Returning to *Halladale*, the passenger lounge just added to the foredeck is noticeable, and one motor coach brings up the rear of this band of Calais bound motorists.

168. MV PRINCE PHILIPPE

Belgian Marine's input to the Dover services was considerable. They were one of the first local ferry operators to put their faith into motor powered ships. Here in 1950, we see their *Prince Philippe* 3,700g/1948 built, departing Dover. This design had first been seen in the 1930s and one distinctive feature of Belgian Marine vessels was the large bridge wing lookout shelters - nearly the size of the central wheelhouse, itself. Perched on the breakwater beyond is the 5000 ton coal bunker awaiting demolition.

169. SS MAID OF ORLEANS (2) →

Another popular ship on the Dover Strait, this 3,777g/1949 built vessel, was the second to carry the name. Apparent just after WWII, is the increasing application of 'streamlining' by the naval architects. Despite being a conventional steamer, this ship has a much shortened funnel, in comparison to the pre-war designs. Powered by four steam turbines, the Denny of Dumbarton tradition continued.

170. MV COMPIEGNE →

French Railways (SNCF) put this ferry into service in 1958 and the 3,467grt vessel clearly shows the stern door arrangements, which would soon become universal. A small after-facing wheelhouse and a 'docking' radar have been fitted, for those frequent astern moves to the linkspan berths. However, the ship's stern door is still relatively small, as heavy freight vehicles had yet to appear in today's size and numbers. Most freight still travelled by separate cargo steamer.

171. MV STEYNING

Dover's commercial docks still handled a brisk conventional coastwise and short sea trade until just a few decades ago. Here, Stephenson, Clarke's motor collier *Steyning* 1,637g/ 1955 has just discharged her coal cargo. This ship, and sister vessel *Lancing* were most often to be found on the gasworks coal run from Goole to Shoreham at this time, but voyages to other ports made some variety, for the collier crews. Later, *Steyning* moved to the Irish Sea coal trade as *Ballywalter*.

172. MT DILIGENT →

When first introduced by P.K.Harris of Apple-dore Shipyard, this design of tug seemed quite radical. A whole series of similar tugs were turned out in the late 1950s and 1960s, and they were most successful. Dover Harbour's pair were *Diligent* and *Dominant* both 161g/1957. The twin diesel uptakes formed the after legs of a neat, radar bearing, tripod mast arrangement.

173. MT PASS OF DALVEEN →

One of the earliest operators in the growing coastal oil distribution trade last century, was the Bulk Oil Steam Ship Company, who started before WWI. In the late 1950s a programme of ship replacement began to thin out their venerable steam tankers. *Pass of Dalveen* 965g/1968 is seen here still bearing the company's distinctive purple and white banded funnel marking. Soon, the ships would be merged into the Cory Group. In this scene from around 1960, the eastern breakwater now carries oil pipes in the absence of the old colliery bunker paraphernalia.

174. MV LUISE HORN

The West German fleet of Heinrich C.Horn was into the refrigerated and perishable foodstuff trade. Here, *Luise Horn* 887g/1961 is entering Dover's Western Docks in part discharged state. It was quite common for ships of this type to unload small consignments of fruit or vegetables, from the Mediterranean or Canary Isles, at more than one destination port. More recently a larger specialist terminal for ocean going 'reefer' ships opened at the Eastern end of the Harbour.

175. MV FREE ENTERPRISE III →

A 1969 view of this bow and stern loading motor ferry 4,657g/1966, makes an interesting comparison to earlier tonnage. *FEI*, *FEII* and *FEIII*, really did point the way forward to the higher superstructure tonnage commonplace today. Freight vehicles were growing individually larger and, multiplying numerically. It is difficult to believe now that at less than 5,000 tons apiece, these ships were the largest on the cross-Channel car ferry routes, at the time of their introduction. Townsend certainly set the pace.

176. Hovercraft - PRINCESS MARGARET →

The development of the large passenger and car carrying hovercraft seems to have peaked in the late 1960s. British Rail had been quick to introduce their service from Dover's Western Docks to Calais and Boulogne. Initially the SRN4 craft carried some 259 passengers plus 35 cars, but after lengthening, the figures rose to 390, plus 55 respectively. All carried at a service speed of 50kts. By the year 2000, harsh economics, fierce competition and the age of the hovercraft conspired to their demise. Today, the only hovercraft service for passengers in the UK is the ten minute Southsea to Ryde, Isle of Wight route, run by Hovertravel.

177. Hovercraft - INGENIEUR JEAN BERTIN

French Railways contribution to the Dover hover service was this high tail-planed Sedam 500 type. Seen on the apron at Dover around 1980, the design incorporated the propellers right aft. A rather 'ship-like' midships mast also differs from the British Rail types, the stern of one being visible alongside the terminal building.

178. MV STENA INVICTA →

Seen here in 1990, the intervening years' effect on ship size and tonnage is very apparent. This largely stems from the phenomenal growth in trans-European, heavy road freight haulage, and the necessity to accommodate these 'juggernaut' trucks onboard. *Stena Invicta* 19,763g/1985 is undoubtedly an efficient carrier, but somehow the grace of the earlier ferries is lacking. However, speed of turnaround, and economy of operation are now the main criteria.

179. MV SEAFRANCE NORD PAS DE CALAIS →

Built as a combined rail and road truck ferry, the 13,727g/1987 built ship is of a design 'light years' from the old steam train ferries. Up to 2400 tons of railway wagon freight may be carried or 1400 tons of road vehicles on the decks. Apart from the twin funnel concept there is little comparison to the 1916 'TFs', or the *Shepperton* types of 1936. The ship has access at bow and stern and the word *Seafrance* was added to her name around 1996.

180. MV SEACAT DIAMANT

The departure of the hovercraft has seen replacement in the form of various high speed mono-hull and catamaran types on the fast services. In this 2005 photograph *Seacat Diamant* 4,305g/1996 is leaving the linkspan berth at the old hovercraft site, by the Prince of Wales Pier. This particular vessel is one of a number of 'hi-speed multi-hull' Incat type craft, built in Australia. They have proven especially handy at coping with seasonal summer traffic on many routes in Europe, as only cars can be handled.

181. MV ASTOR →

Dover has become a busy cruise ship port in recent years and now two such berths are available along the old Admiralty Pier to handle this traffic. In this 2005 scene *Astor* 20,606g/1987 is at the inner berth, adjacent to the old Dover Marine Station. She is operated by Transocean Tours of Bremen, principally in the German cruise market, and can accommodate 590 passengers.

182. MV PALOMA I →

In the next berth to No.181, is the small Polish built cruise ship *Paloma I* , 12,586 gross tons. She can handle 354 passengers, and is similarly Bremen based. Although these two are very small by modern cruise ship standards, it is interesting to note that tonnages of many current cross-Channel ferries far exceed those of some ocean liners, from a half century ago.

183.   Road freight has won.

The 2005 view across the Folkestone railway line surely highlights the vast changes hereabouts over the last two hundred years. From simple beginnings the port has evolved through the railway era with its 'boat trains' connecting capital to capital, and the bustle of commercial shipping in the Western Docks, the train ferry and the car ferry era, and modern road freight handling. The hovercraft came and went in relatively short order, cruise ships have arrived in a big way, and even Dover has joined the ever growing list of yacht marinas around our coasts. In the photograph, the commercial basins now house yachts and in the foreground not a single railway siding remains in place, where the tarmac truck marshalling area now sits. Thankfully, Dover Castle still presides from on high, and the foreground detail makes for a fascinating comparison to that of No.149

184. The Eastern Docks

This 2005 view may be compared to No.167, although from a different angle. In the present day scene, an assortment of large roll-on, roll-off ferries go about their daily job of extending Europe's motorways across the Channel, a twenty four-hour activity. From left to right can be seen:

Speed-one	Speedlines 'Incat' fast ferry	
Pride of Acquitaine *	P&O	28,883g/1991
Pride of Burgundy	P&O	28,138g/1993 (underway)
Seafrance Manet	Seafrance	15,093g/1984
Seafrance Cezanne	Seafrance	24,122g/1986

This ship shortly left Dover to join LD Lines Portsmouth to Le Havre route vacated by P&O in autumn 2005. New name- *Norman Spirit*.

Map No. 11   Folkestone Harbour

(1)   Folkestone, Inner Harbour
(2)   Approximate site of the Channel Tunnel Terminal
(3)   End of the Royal Military Canal, Hythe

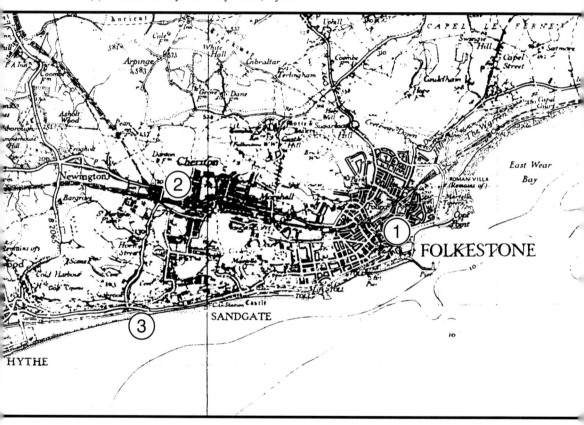

Folkestone

Folkestone developed from a small fishing village in the 18th century, with some coasting and French trade. In 1766 a duty imposed on coal imports, enabled maintenance to be carried out on the simple wooden pier infrastructure. In one respect the harbour benefited from littoral drift, the eastward movement of shingle along the English Channel coast, as it built up against a stone groyne. This naturally assisted in the later development of the Harbour. Around 1809, the engineer Telford carried out some improvement works, but not with undue success. In 1843, the South Eastern Railway Company bought the harbour, and duly the first steamer left for Boulogne.

Passenger trains were allowed down the steep branch to the harbour in 1848, some time after goods traffic started. At this time the Harbour Station was situated immediately beyond the swing bridge and it would be 1876 before trains could run right out along the pier, enabling direct access to the steamers for passengers, luggage and mails. In the late 1800s, locally owned sailing ships were active in the coal and coasting trades. 1893 saw the construction of the second, stronger swing bridge to cope with ever heavier trains.

Between WWI and 1926, the Dutch owned Zeeland Shipping Company ran their steamers from Folkestone to Flushing, but finally opted for Harwich as their only UK terminal. In 1930, the present swing bridge, came into service.

Steamer services at this time were:
Passengers

	Boulogne	twice daily
	Dunkirk	every weekday night
Cargo ships	same destinations	daily

In the 1950s, the traditional general cargo steamer services from the old outer harbour ended. SS *Deal* was one of the last so employed. The 1970s and 1980s saw an ever decreasing number of railway generated passengers. British Rail built a linkspan berth to accept their two new roll-on, roll-off car ferries Hengist and *Horsa* both 5,590g/1972. These ships could carry 1400 passengers, 210 cars, or 38 trucks each. The route and ships would ultimately pass over to Sealink control, on privatisation.

By 1998, Hoverspeed and Falcon Seafreights were sailing from the port and in 1999 the two ships present were *Purbeck*, and *Picasso*. Around 2001, the terminal closed and the linkspan removed. A couple of miles inland, the Channel Tunnel Terminal now reigns supreme as Folkestone's continental point of entry.

185.   Folkestone Harbour around 1900

Local fishing craft put out to sea on a calm day, as a boat train climbs up to the main line. Between the 1893 swing bridge, and the entrance, can be seen two white funnelled railway steamers and a small steam coaster, close to the bridge. To the left, moored stern on to the embankment wall, lays another old cargo steamer and a barquentine. Through the haze, out along the 'S' shape of the pier and station, funnels of passenger ferries can just be picked out, in all, a lively bustling scene.

186.   CYPRESS and the Royal Pavilion Hotel

A variety of sailing traders may be seen here in front of the splendid Royal Pavilion Hotel. With flag flying high, a Scandinavian two masted schooner is in the basin corner, beyond a deeply laden ketch. The distinctive black and white hulled brigantine in the foreground is the *Cypress* 211r/1860, a Sunderland built wooden ship, owned at this time by Mr. R.G. Sanders of Folkestone.

187.   SCOTIA of Folkestone

Seen here in 1908 probably awaiting the opening of the swing bridge to gain access to the inner harbour is another local ship. She is the Folkestone owned barquentine *Scotia* 291r/1873 and is being steadied by a kedge anchor, while the crew await the swinging of the bridge. A large number of people appear to be thronging the quayside nearby, where one of the 1896-1905 batch of railway cargo steamers is berthed. With a big ketch over to the right and other tall masts visible, Folkestone was indeed showing its diversity of shipping and trade.

188. SS MECKLENBURG

Zeeland Shipping's *Mecklenburg* 2,998g/1922 worked the Folkestone to Flushing night service between WWI and 1926. At that point the company left Kent completely, never to return, and made Harwich their terminal. This fine old steamer served her owners well for over forty years. Twin quadruple expansion engines gave a speed of 22 knots - certainly as fast as many of the railway turbine steamers of the day.

189. SS MAID OF ORLEANS (1) →

We have already seen the later ship of the same name. This is the 1918 version, 1,676grt and built for the South Eastern & Chatham Railway, she is already up to quite a 'clip' as she heads out for Boulogne. A 24kt ship, she shows the start of better weather protection for passengers, with closed in side alleyways.

190. SS MAIDSTONE →

Although seen here crossing Dover Harbour in the 1950s, this ship is a good example of the final class of Southern Railway cargo steamers built. At 686g/1926 she, and a number of sister vessels, ran on numerous railway ferry routes in tandem with the more 'glamorous' passenger ships. At a sedate 12kts service speed all forms of general goods were carried, usually to a daily timetable.

191. SS COTE D'AZUR

French Railways, (SNCF), put this streamlined turbine steamer into service in 1951. Of 3,998grt, she would be a popular stalwart on the Folkestone to Boulogne route for many years. The classic passenger only ferries were certainly more graceful than today's truck carrying giants, and speeds have fallen back over the years from a peak of 22 to 24 knots, to the region of 18 to 22 knots. The 'surface effect' type fast ferries can of course, manage well over 40 knots service speed.

192. MV HORSA →

Horsa and sister ship *Hengist* 5,590g/72 still managed to retain some degree of earlier design elegance, despite their roll-on, roll-off type. No longer in British Rail's livery, in this photograph *Horsa* is moving astern to that other indispensable modern item, the linkspan berth facility. These two ships carried 1400 passengers, and 210 cars apiece, and marked a period when through passengers by rail were becoming scarcer. This led to the end for traditional boat trains and passenger only ships.

193. The 1930 Swingbridge →

The railways' third version stands across the access to the inner harbour, and now looks a little 'tired' in 2005. Various cables and service pipes dangle from it, and there has been no necessity for opening for a long time; its permanent closure is a formality.

← 194. HAPPY RETURN FE5

Festooned with bunting and open to the public one day in July 2005, is the magnificently restored fishing lugger, *Happy Return*. Built at Porthleven in 1904, she is one survivor of a type that once numbered thousands around our coasts and would not have warranted a second glance. In earlier years this lugger is believed to have worked out of Folkestone, so the FE5 registration number is appropriate.

195. The Pier in 2005

One hundred and sixty two years after the first steamer left for Boulogne, the berths that have witnessed so much frantic activity in the interim are now silent. The roll-on, roll-off gantry remains from the last vehicle ferry operation, but the linkspan has been removed. Peace pervades the berths, station and remaining rail line and surely it is to be hoped that some worthwhile project can re-vitalise this once famously traditional port of entry. See No.188 for the earlier similar view.

196. THV PENLEE →

Trinity House Pilot Vessels, such as *Penlee* 443g/1948, were stationed well off shore in a number of locations around the United Kingdom coastline. Pilots would be put aboard incoming merchantmen heading for the country's major ports, and taken off again, outbound. In this 1950s photograph, the ship has her transfer boarding launch swung out ready for action. Accommodation was provided onboard for several pilots who had to await their incoming ship rota, before returning ashore to their families. Usually, the ships were out 'on station' for a week at a time, as in the case off Dungeness. By the 1970s, most such pilot vessels had been replaced by fast launch services direct from shore bases to the incoming and outgoing merchant ships. Naturally, this method of operation would be more economic and socially acceptable for all concerned.

Map No.12 Dungeness Point

    (1) Old Pilot Station   (2) Lighthouses at the Point

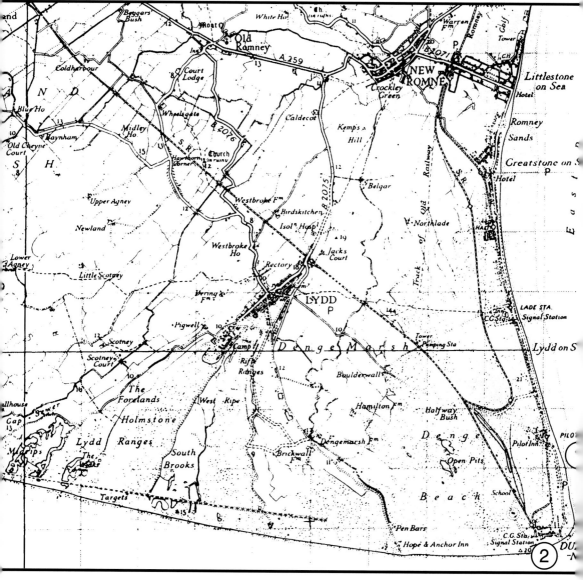

197. SS HACKNEY

With Dungeness power stations a planner's distant dream, here the Central Electricity Authority steam collier *Hackney* 1,782g/1952 steams round the Point in the 1950s. She was of the up-river, Thames 'flat-iron' coal brigade, and likely here to be on a run from South Wales. By no means did all of London's coal come from the North East of England. The solitary lighthouse dating from 1904 can be seen above the shingle beach.

198. MV KINDRENCE

This 1980 image is included to illustrate just how diverse the old London & Rochester Trading Company had become. Now known as Crescent Shipping, the *Kindrence* 1,596g/1976 is seen proudly showing the 'crescent' emblem on her funnel. Together with a sister vessel, *Luminence*, the two ships undertook power station coal runs, as the last of the old Electricity Authority steam colliers were phased out. The ship is seen departing Shoreham and within a couple more decades the Company would decide to shift operations to coastal tankers, as is the case today. From sailing barges to coastal cargo ships, thence tankers - long may it prosper!

199. Dungeness Lighthouses in 1904 →

Our voyage around Kent terminates hereabouts, as indeed so does Kent, just a few miles to the west. That old familiar littoral shingle drift manifests itself no more spectacularly than at Dungeness Point. Around six feet of extra shingle per year can accumulate. In this image a new lighthouse has just been built, and the earlier 1792 version awaits demolition on the right.

200. The 1960 Light Tower

Made necessary by the nearby construction of the first Dungeness Power Station, this modern style reinforced concrete ring structure is, as one would come to expect, totally automatic. At 130ft above sea level, a white light flashes every ten seconds, and is visible twenty seven miles away at sea. The 'fog-horn' perforations can be seen just below the gallery, and the old 1904 tower is now in 'retirement' black and open for tourists in summer. Views are phenomenal, for those keen on the spiral stairway!

An aside - overheard on many a ship's bridge in days gone by:
- We have dropped the Pilot, rounded Dungeness Point and
set course down Channel -

"Tell the Engine Room to work up to full sea speed, and Full Away On Passage
(F.A.O.P.) will be rung on the telegraph, on the hour"

The deep sea passage begins, the coastal one ends - as does this book.

Bibliography

Sailorman between the Wars	John Allendale	1978	-------------------
South Eastern Sail	Michael Bouquet	1972	0 7153 559 29
Richborough Port	R.Butler	1999	0 9531 801 15
Sailing Barges	Martin Hazel	1976	0 8526 333 43
A History of the Southern Railway	C.F.Dendy Marshall	1936	-------------------
Maritime Thanet	Robert B.Matkin	1982	-------------------
Ports of the United Kingdom	Owen, Sir David J.	1939	--------------------
Shipwreck, Broken on the Wight	Ken Phillips	1995	1 8981 980 71
Oysters and Dredgermen	Geoffrey Pike	1992	0 9509 984 43
The Last Berth of the Sailormen-			
The Society for Sailing Barge Research		1996	0 9500 515 6X
Kent & East Sussex Waterways	P.A.L.Vine	1989	0 9065 207 2X

Lloyds Registers
Mercantile Navy Lists
World Ship Society- Marine News
Shipping Magazines
Local Newspapers

INDEX

Acknowledgements

I would like to record thanks and appreciation to all the kind individuals, societies and organisations, who with their time, information and material, have so helped in the compilation of this book in particular: Jonathan Balkwill, Bob Bradley, Tony Carder, Michael Child, Alan Cordell, Norma Crowe, Judith Dore, Paul Dummott, Keith Elliott, Tony Farnham, Manda Gifford, Harold Gough, Ray Harlow, Michael Hunt, Norman Langridge, Magdalena Mayo, Vic Mitchell, Peter Morgan, Phil Neumann, Arthur Percival MBE, Bob Ratcliffe, Peter Stevens, Lynn Vine (Queenborough Guildhall Museum), David Whiteside and Elizabeth Wood.

Photographic sources

Alan Cordell collection 59
Deal Maritime and Local History Museum 139
East Kent Maritime Museum, Ramsgate 114,118,128,129
Elgate Products Ltd 119,127
The Environment Agency 10
The Faversham Society 64,66,70,71,72,73
Fotoflite 31,46,47,48,82,103,104,145,146,160,161,168,178,179,196,197
The Francis Frith Collection 80
Herne Bay Historical Records Society 90
Kent Messenger 30
Margate Museum 94,97,101
Medway Archive and Local Studies Centre 18
Michaels Bookshop (Ramsgate) Map 8.1
Bob Ratcliffe collection 20
Sandwich Guildhall Museum 136,137
Science and Society Picture Library 93
Sheerness Heritage Centre 51
Sittingbourne Heritage Society 53,57,58
Sittingbourne and Kemsley Light Railway 54
The Society for Sailing Barge Research, Walter Dowsett collection 6,8,9
Whitstable Museum and Gallery, Douglas West collection 77
World Ship Society-Photo Library, 17,91,147,148,161,162,163, 164,165

Ordnance Survey maps are from the 1930s, one inch to one mile scale.

MP Middleton Press

EVOLVING THE ULTIMATE RAIL ENCYCLOPEDIA

Easebourne Lane, Midhurst, West Sussex.
GU29 9AZ   Tel:01730 813169

www.middletonpress.co.uk   email:info@middletonpress.co.uk

A-0 906520   B-1 873793   C-1 901706   D-1 904474

OOP Out of Print at time of printing - Please check current availability   **BROCHURE AVAILABLE SHOWING NEW TITLES**